Humans 1st
Students 2nd

Humans 1st Students 2nd

Berry Best Books
Publishing Co.

Book cover design by Berry Best Publishing LLC Editing:

Kyonna Hardy

February 2024, First Edition ISBN 979-8218-3785-61

An Imprint of Berry Best Publishing LLC
www.berrybestpublishing.com

Ordering Information:
Available through Amazon, Barnes and Noble, and Kindle. & www.restorativerecipes.com. Special discounts are available on quantity purchases by corporations, associations, educators, and others. For details, contact the publisher at the above listed address.

Humans 1st
Students 2nd

Cultivating & Sustaining Meaningful
Relationships through Restorative
Practices

A Guide For Educators

Kyonna Hardy

Dedication

I dedicate this book to my mother who has supported me in insurmountable ways during this journey.

I dedicate this book to my Teacher Squad, particularly my Team9 team who followed my lead despite the chaos or unconventional methods. You validated me and trusted me as you allowed me to lead in some of the best years of my educational career.

I dedicate this to all my Restorative Warriors. From the principal who encouraged me to take the trainings and then supported me in the implementation at the school, all the way to One Hand Up.

Last but never least, I dedicate this book to my babies, aka the students, particularly from SVAH, who helped me more than they know, become the change I wanted to see.

Table of Contents

Foreward

—

In the almost 18 years I have been in education, ranging from Pre-K all the way through 12th grade, I have encountered some of the best of the best teachers as well as the not-so great. But each one of those people along my journey taught me great lessons and really helped shape me into the educator, and more deeply, the human, that I am today.

It is funny how sometimes who you are naturally aligned with an outcome or expectation, and I would say that who I am naturally and what I care about most, seamlessly aligns with what it means to be 'restorative'. Of course, I did not know this at the beginning of my teaching journey, but once the restorative movement became the new "buzz", I finally was able to define myself in an educational sense.

I was, and still am, a culturally aware as well as responsive, restorative educator. And despite leaving the classroom, my 'why' was, and still very much is, rooted in molding my students into better human beings. Although 'English teacher' was my title while in the classroom, I was definitely much more than that. Therefore, in the last few years of my time as a class- room teacher, I equated my curriculum to side with more of a Humanities or Ethnic Studies course (both of which are electives but should definitely be a requirement in high

. . . .

school-but that's another conversation).

So, what does it mean to be 'restorative'? Well, restorative principles are rooted in the philosophy that the human race is extremely interconnected, and that the collective well-being of the community takes precedence over individual needs or wants. No one is thought of as being naturally troubled, but instead, circumstances cause trauma. And Relationships are paramount. Reminds me of an African proverb that I enjoy using in trainings: "I Am Because We Are."

This Ubuntu philosophy places an emphasis on "being self through others". To me, we are all uniquely individual, as there is not one other single person on this planet that is who you or me are (even for those that share the same DNA). But within that unique individuality, holds the responsibility to know that who we are is because of others and that we should feel morally obligated to make sure that others are considered in our day- to-day decisions. It is sometimes a difficult concept to grasp. Some of us value competition, individual results, and the need to always be number #1. After all, America instills these ideologies in us from a very young age- especially in the school system. However, when you shift your mindset to be more aware of the group, taking time to care about the next person, amazing things will happen. Not only in your classroom, the school environment, or the surrounding community, but in your life as a whole.

. . . .

In order to live restoratively, you have to understand the power of forming relationships and know that relationships are at the center. According to the International Institute of Restorative Practices (IIRP), "All humans are hardwired to connect. Just as we need food, shelter, and clothing, human beings also need strong and meaningful relationships to thrive." But building significant and authentic relationships with others definitely takes time and patience. With this in mind, ultimately, the goal is to form these types of relationships through the values of mutual respect and effective communication. All great relationships need these two things, especially in a restorative environment. Sadly, the majority of our youth may not have ever had an example, direct or indirect, of what a healthy relationship looks like. With social media being what it is, coupled with already existing traumas, or what society characterizes as "gender norms", such as phrases like "boys will be boys" or "don't be a sissy", our youth face complex challenges while trying to navigate these ideals alone. And so, the cycle of toxic relationships between friends, peers, romantic partners, and the individual and society, continues to circulate because no one took the time to show and guide them differently. But you, however, should be that one adult in their life that can show them another way, a different perspective. There is not much that we can control when it comes down to our students' lives- but we have all the control on the type of classroom environment we create for them and the relationships we build with them.

"Traditional soil" of the educational school system is rooted in obedience, compliance, and conformity. In elementary schools, students are to raise their hands (which I am NOT a fan of at all) and to walk in lines usually with their hands behind their backs (also not a fan of because it can be quite criminalizing). When they get to middle school, which we all know is a time of vast changes both physically, mentally, and emotionally, more freedom is allotted to students, but there is also more responsibility. So, adults spend their time trying to control and dominate students by creating rigid rules and extremely harsh consequences. So, by the time they reach high school, most students are scorned or have developed a sense of rebellion against the system as they are given even more responsibility and applied pressure to perform at higher standards to complete assignments or tasks that they see no value or use for in their present-day life or future. Case in point-No offense to my brilliant mathematicians, but when was the last time you used the Pythagorean theorem?

So school, as an institution, is not seen as a safe, happy place that most kids eagerly wake up in the morning to attend. But instead, it is compared to a prison where every moment of a student's day is controlled and dictated by someone else in an authoritative role-usually an adult and the clock. And sadly, some schools resemble prisons too. Where I grew up, a fence surrounds every school, and most with either hooks at the top or barbwire. The buildings lack color, and some don't even have windows. Staff members stand guard at the entrances, and more than a handful of schools even have metal detectors. And the school police division has a designated office on campus. All of this contributes to a broken system – a system that within its current way of doing things simply does not work, in which statistics nationally have proven.

I remember one year, while teaching, almost every week, there was a "random" search of classrooms with portable metal detectors and dogs. Dogs! Administration and the school officer would storm into the classroom unannounced and begin plucking students up out of their learning environment to go outside, place their hands on the wall, surrender their items, and not speak. Now mind you, I understand that school safety is of extreme importance. And depending on where you live, you may have to take certain precautions that another campus may not have to. However, we all know the 3-tiered pyramid of student behavior. 80% of your students are making the "right" choices, focusing on their schoolwork, navigating life as best they can without any major disruptions-that's our base. In the middle, our 10-15% percent of students are going to need some extra support as they struggle with their decisions all while maintaining a sense of purpose of self. And then we will have that final 1-5% at the peak that will need more than just support. They will need support, resources, and interventions. But that should not impede or negatively affect the lives of the other 85-90%. That pyramid should not be turned on its head. But sadly, traditionally, schools function in exactly this way: Upside-down. Rule-governed. And extremely Punitive.

This book will provide personal anecdotes and reflective questions as to help sow seeds in your soul and then assist you in the creation of new soil; new soil that your students can plant themselves in and grow into beautiful roses—even if concrete is continuously poured on top of them by circumstances outside of your and their control. But this new soil is for you too because you are human too. And human first, just like our students. Which is why I always say, this work is *about* the kids, but it is *for* the adults. But this work requires a true paradigm shift in thinking.

So despite all the odds stacked against your students as well as yourself, still, your soil should be so rich that it encourages, fosters, and cultivates the development of beautiful roses to grow though the concrete (shout out Tupac Shakur) and show the world that the faith of a mustard seed prevails despite it all.

Despite What 'They' Say, Smile. Please. Always. August

—

I remember my first day of teaching as if it was yesterday. I was a fresh 23, teaching at a high school campus where I used to be a student. (Which made for some future trippy staff parties... but those are stories for another book). I was overjoyed because my alma mater gave me my first shot at making a splash in the waters of the teaching world, so I was determined to make the best of it and become the best first-year teacher the district had ever seen.

Unfortunately, from the beginning, it did not quite turn out that way. Just weeks before I was to sign my official contract, there was a hiring freeze; which meant I was unable to sign, thus leaving me as a long-term substitute-subbing for myself, in the position I was hired for. That's right. Every morning, I would get a sub sheet with my schedule and attendance password that said, 'Sub for Kyonna Hardy'. This lasted for yeaaarrrsss. But that, again, is another story.

So, I began my teaching career essentially how we all do: determined to change the world, one student at a time, all bright-eyed and bushy-tailed, eager to build a teacher squad who shared your same vision and mindset.

But that magical bubble burst the day I went into the teacher's cafeteria.

It was the third day of school-which happened to be a Friday, because we had started school in the middle of the week. Undoubtedly, I was excited to have survived my first week and felt brave enough to venture beyond the walls of my own classroom. So, I traveled across campus to the teacher's cafeteria. There, in the back, was a table. And at this table, was probably 150 years plus of teaching experience combined, eating their overpriced cafeteria meals, discussing the day. Of course, I knew better to sit at that table, because I felt like I had to go through some type of initiation first-some type of 'Rite of Passage'. But I did sit close, because you are told in your teaching programs to soak up the wisdom of those older and "wiser" than you. I couldn't really hear what they were saying, but I remained there until the bell rang indicating lunch was over. With eyes still on the "vet table", I got up, smiled in their direction, and began to walk towards the hall. But before I could pass the trashcan, one of the "old wise ones" came over to me and said, verbatim:

"You're one of the new teachers, right? Well, let me give you a word of advice. Never, and I mean never, let students see you smile."

I nervously laughed at this bit of "wisdom" and said, "I will keep that in mind," as I scurried away from him. Such a comment threw me for a loop; and although I never really followed it, it always lingered in the back of my mind. The result, I would say then, in my first year of teaching, I almost rebelled against the advice. I made it my mission to smile all the time, get in all my students' business, and really become a part of their day-to-day. I listened to their stories and even took their suggestions for the day's lesson, although I was simultaneously attempting to follow the script provided to me by the District to the letter. I became what most first-year teachers become: Permissive. I met the needs and supported my students in all the social-emotional ways, but I lacked boundaries and high expectations. And so, I stayed in the lower right corner of the Social Window box[1] for probably the first three years of my teaching career. I became the "popular teacher", the "chill teacher", "the easy grader", and the "let you do whatever teacher". That was who I was in the beginning of my teaching career: a permissively smiling "equal", allowing the students to dictate their education, but not in a way that you would want.

Now don't get me wrong. I cherish those first batches of babies. Because there is a lesson to be learned in every 'L' that you take. And it wasn't until later in life that I realized the impact that I had on the lives of those students that, for some, I still keep in contact today. It was the little personable things that I did, such as buy an organizer, or write positive affirmations on sticky notes each week, or just provide that safe space for students to come and hang out. So, I take great pride in creating those connections, but it wasn't until I moved to a social

. . . .

justice interdisciplinary project-based learning visual art pilot school that I truly began to evolve into the amazing, influential, restorative educator that I am still. It was there that I moved from permissive to restorative in the Social Window. I gained the phenomenal teacher squad that I needed. That I understood what it really meant to build connections and relationships with my students that would last a lifetime. That I began to establish my legacy.

---

1 Social Discipline Window or Relationship Matrix describes four basic approaches to maintaining social norms and behavioral boundaries. The four are represented as different combinations of high or low control and high or low support.
Refer to Figure 1

. . . .

10

Shared Experience Moment

Think of a time when you were excited about something that was brand new to you.

- Did you study and take advice from the "experts"?

- Did you blaze your own path without influence?

- What lessons did you take from your decisions and overall experience?

- How did this experience help you grow and in what ways?

Which attitude in the Social Window would you place yourself when you first started teaching? Along your journey? Currently?

If you are not where you would like to be, what steps can you take to get to that level? And if you are, what are you going to continue to do to keep you there?

Figure 1: Social Discipline Window

High Expectations	DOING TO	DOING WITH
	Stigmatizing	*Collaborative*
	Blaming	*Accountable*
	Harsh	*Problem-solving*
	Authoritarian	*Positive*
	Confrontational	*Connected*
	Punitive	*Restorative*
Low Expectations	DOING NOTHING	DOING FOR
	Uninvolved	Naïve
	Ignoring	Excusing
	Indifferent	Rescuing
	Lazy	Laissez-Faire
	Neglectful	Permissive
	Low Support	High Support

The top-left stands for an authoritarian approach where there is high control, but low support. This sets rules and rig- idly holds people to them, with little room for explanation.

The bottom left is low in support and also low in expectations. This can be potentially dangerous because this box represents not doing anything.

The bottom right is low in expectations, but high in support. This approach sometimes allows for poor choices to go unchecked because no clear expectations are set.

The box where both expectations and support are high is in the Restorative Box. This is where you should strive to be. This approach sets boundaries, but also nurtures the individual and provides the support to accomplish the goal.

The matrix can reveal the gaps in expectations and/or support.

This window is also fluid-just like the 3-tiered pyramid. No one stays in one quadrant 100% of the time, especially when handling conflict

Restorative Recipe #1
You Have to Build Your
Classroom Family

—

If there was anything that I learned in my first permissive few years of teaching, it was the importance of human connection.

I realized how much those connections could mean to someone, and if I wanted to have my students conquer the top tier of Maslow's Hierarchy of Needs (Self-Actualization), then I would need to make sure that each one of my students knew that I saw them as *humans first, students second*.

In recognizing their humanity, prior to them arriving, I made sure that my room was aesthetically pleasing. Bright colored butcher paper for the boards. Inspiring Quotes. Culturally- Relevant Posters. A Calming Corner (yes, even in high school). Community table with supplies. My own personalized teacher's corner. And my favorite: a 'Wall of Wisdom' with messages from the previous year's students.

I truly cannot express the importance of making your classroom an environment that someone wouldn't mind spending their time. Think about some of your favorite places. What about the set-up do you enjoy so much? Is there music playing when you come in? Are the colors soothing or vibrant? Does someone immediately greet you with a smile and call you by name? Are there people there that you recognize and happy to share space with? Do you just feel good there and even better when you leave?

If you answered yes to any of these questions, then you know the importance of setting up your classroom in a way that will have students answering yes to each of the above-mentioned questions as well. And if you are familiar with PBIS, then you know that 'Maximizing your Class Structure' is number 1 of the 5 components. Thus, I cannot emphasize the point enough that your classroom climate matters! The National Center for School Climate, defines climate as the "quality and character of school life." It's not something separate, which means your classroom is not just your own, but an integral part of the fabric of the school community, which establishes the culture. Climate stems from the relationships that exist between and among students, staff, faculty, family, and the community at large. But remember that the climate wavers- depending on multiple factors such as testing, who's absent or not, the time of year, cultural events, etc.

And speaking of PBIS for a moment, I want to clarify that PBIS and Restorative are NOT the same. But they do complement each other quite well. In one of my favorite restorative books, *Better than Carrots or Sticks, Restorative Practices for Positive Classroom Management*, it outlines the two most important aspects of creating an effective learning environment: relationships and high-quality instruction, while distinguishing the difference between the two. SW (schoolwide) PBIS provides schools with a means for evaluating student behaviors and identifying function, eliminating the conditions that trigger unwanted behaviors, and teaching replacement behaviors. [Whereas] the restorative approach to discipline incorporates principles of SWPBIS approach to focus on prevention through relationship building by drawing on the collective strengths of the community to help individuals in trouble regain their footing in a nurturing environment with consistent classroom practices and high expectations.[2] Each of these should not exist without the other if your goal is to be a restorative educator cultivating a restorative community.

So, for the first 2 ½ weeks of school, I developed the 'We are Family' Unit. A unit that focused solely on our class com- munity, setting up ourselves as a Team 9 family and learning each one of us as an individual. This is something that I strongly recommend that you do for those first few weeks. Do not-and I repeat *DO NOT*- have the first day with your students be you standing in front of the class going over the syllabus. This is the fastest way to lose your students for the rest of the year. You will lose that magical opportunity to show to each one of your students that you are not like any of their teachers past; but instead, that you could be that one adult that could forever make a difference in their life, beyond

. . . .

academics.

Here's how I did it:

For August, I offer the following blueprint. This will lay the foundation and implement Tier I strategies that are necessary for optimal success.

1. 10 days of community-building activities
   a. Getting to Know You/Interest survey
   b. Seating Activities
   c. Name Game *(knowing names communicates value and importance)*
   d. Establish the Classroom Expectations together as a class
   e. Respect Agreement Figure 1.2
   f. Icebreakers
   g. Connect with the Classroom Activities
   h. What Kind of Learner are You? Activities

---

2 Better than Carrots or Sticks, Restorative Practices for Positive Classroom Management. 18-19

Laying this solid foundation is critical the first couple of weeks of school. Not only are the students building connections with their peers in addition to you, but those first 10 days allow you to learn more about your students' personalities, level of social skills, and possibly some fun facts you may have not learned until much later. Knowing these factors soon will help you tremendously because you will no longer be creating seating charts or forming groups without intentionality because you will now have more information about each student beyond assumptions or generalizations.

In fact, restorative practices should dwell in any and all aspects of the school, especially within social interactions. Taking the time out to build community in the beginning will save you possibly months of dealing with disruptive behaviors—Trust Me.

The Journey Begins...
August Still

—

When I decided to teach at the pilot school, I was still considered a long-term sub. The District was going through furloughs (such a hard time in education) and so I was one of the first to lose my position. So, when the opportunity to secure another long-term position came shortly after getting Rif'd (Won't He Do It!), I jumped at the opportunity.

My interview was set for 7 pm on a Wednesday night, about 15 miles from my home. I arrived at 6:45 pm at a historical landmark (it was the old *Ambassador Hotel-* yeah that one- where Robert F. Kennedy was assassinated). As I walked up the stairs to the third floor, I was excited and intrigued, because the school setup was different from any traditional high school I had ever been to. So immediately, I felt like I was going to be a part of something special. By the time I reached the third floor, I had passed three other pilot schools, which only heightened my curiosity and desire to be a part of something so innovative and unorthodox. I made it to the office, and it was dark just one light source beaming from underneath a closed door. I sat in the office waiting for about 7 minutes until the administrative assistant- a woman I still hold near and dear to mi Corazon- came to get me and escort me to the room with the light. It was the Principal's office—little did I know that I would be meeting the woman who would help transform my educational approach and mindset. Neither one of us knew it at the time, but she became instrumental in placing me on the path of my restorative teaching journey.

I greeted her with a huge smile, and she returned the same. I sat down and we began to small talk until a very pregnant woman entered the room excitedly. It was then I realized that I was taking over the position of this very pregnant someone; in fact, she was due to give birth just days after my interview. Both women interviewed me for about 30 minutes, and I felt like I had known them in a prior life. I left the office feeling great about the idea of working there and they must have felt similar, because just, 20 minutes later, I received a call from both of them on speaker phone, offering me the position. With resounding joy, I replied, "Yes, of course!" Little did I know I would be starting sooner than any of us would have thought.

The next morning, I received a call from the principal, and she told me that the teacher who was a part of the interview process had gone into labor shortly after our phone call just the night before, therefore I needed to be ready to take over the classroom the next day. Yikes!

Since it was October, I knew that I would be entering an already established culture; one that I knew I would have to adapt to. But I also knew that I would have to create my own culture too. Although this was only my third year teaching, and I may not have known exactly who I was as an educator, but I definitely knew what kind of educator I was not. So, learning the new environment, but most importantly, learning the kids, was top priority for me. However, I did not want to be the permissive teacher of my past nor the authoritarian so many veteran teachers encouraged me to be. Therefore, it was in this class that I developed my own style; a combination of both teacher types, but also with an asterisk. It was in that year that I realized how important it was to respect students as their own human self and understand that they came with a whole set of ideas and life experiences that shaped who they were as an individual. I spent the majority of the school year with those students, and I truly believe that they taught me more than I could ever teach them. Because, finally, I was able to find the balance of building relationships with them while keeping boundaries and still providing them a quality education that consisted of real-life connections and topics ideas and concepts that really mattered to them, not just content that the state mandated for some test.

So, for over 6 months I embraced this newfound sense of identity and once the now "new mommy" teacher returned back to that classroom, I was fortunate enough to stay on that campus in another position that opened itself again to me immediately after. And I was able to remain on that campus to see those 9th graders travel through their educational journey and life's obstacle course all the way to graduation day.

Sadly, not all of them made it. Some got locked up. Some got kicked out. Some moved to another school. Some dropped out of school. But that particular class opened my eyes to the fact that not all students come to school to learn, but to be within those walls eight hours of the day was much better than what was waiting for them on the other side once they walked through those gates. But whatever life had in store for each of those students, their life stories became a part of my own and helped to highlight the path I too was walking on my own life's journey that would take me from a caterpillar to a butterfly in more ways than just teaching.

Shared Experience Moment

Think of a time when you went into a situation believing things were one way, but soon learned that it was not the same as you first thought.

- What were the similarities and/or differences in your thoughts?

- Did you accept the new information, or did you challenge it?

- What lessons did you take from your decisions and overall experience?

- How did you this experience help you grow and in what ways?

Restorative Recipe #2
Build Relationships

—

The amazing Rita Pearson once said that students do not work for people that they don't like, and she is absolutely right about that. As absurd as this sounds to the "traditional" educator, it is beyond important to form strong relationships with each one of your students and for them to create, repair, restore, or rebuild their relationships with one another. As my former business partner and still close friend pledges, 'The Better We Know Each Other, the Better We Are To Each Other". The more we "see" each other as a human, the harder it becomes to be mean, rude, or disrespectful. Only when this is the focal point in your classroom will it then be able to become more than academic lessons and tests. It becomes real-life worthy, and the students will see this and appreciate it because you have to remember that you are NOT teaching your specific content whether that be English, Math, History, or Science— *you are teaching humans*. Therefore, that should be your focus and priority. Some of our kids do not come to school to learn the lesson you stayed up all night planning; but that does not mean that they are incapable of learning. You simply must teach life lessons, which are lessons all students can benefit from, even if you are focusing on a select few.

You cannot exist within this world without having

at least one relationship with someone else. Relationships are unavoidable and inevitable. So, it baffles me that those in upper management or leadership positions sometimes do not see the value in creating and sustaining positive relationships within their communal spaces. Relationships, no matter how shallow or deep, are key to any successful community. But to cultivate positive relationships, you must be intentional about the practices as well as the belief that everyone is capable of contribution and deserving of acceptance. But understand that this is not a sprint, but a marathon. Nothing will happen overnight. But every action in building relationships is like planting a seed. And just like when you plant seeds, you have to nourish and cultivate the soil-which in our case is the school environment- for those seeds to grow and flourish.

The first steps to building authentic relationships are rooted in the restorative practices of community building- all of which, just like Recipe #1- is Tier I implementation- the foundation. And my favorite type of community building practice is community-building circles, or sometimes called proactive circles.[3] But before we dive into the specifics of these types of circles, let me make sure to say that restorative discipline/justice and its practices are NOT a program. There is no special pre-packaged box of lessons or scripts- this is a paradigm shift, a philosophical approach, and a process. And more personally still, to make that shift takes some deep reflection. Therefore, proactive circles should not be thought of as solely a preventative measure that will decrease the likelihood of inappropriate behavior, but it should also be viewed as the cornerstones of setting up meaningful relationships and connections.

Meaningful relationships should also be intentionally created with the parents and/or guardians of your students. Getting them on your side as it takes a village to raise a child- is vital in meeting the needs of the student. Your first interaction should NEVER be a phone call home telling them how horrible their child is. And that will definitely not help with the relationship you need to build with the student either. Instead, you should make positive phone calls home and send home positive notes prior to any negative interaction. Circle with parents is also a great opportunity to build relationships and get to know them on a deeper level. Open House or Coffee with the Principal or other important adult nights present the best opportunities to have such interactions. Think of all of these positive interactions as deposits in the bank, so if and when you need to make a withdrawal, i.e., a talk about inappropriate behaviors, the parent/guardian will be more open to working with you on finding a solution and continuing support.

In my earlier roles, I had Circle with parents once a month. And many of Circle topics were the same their students experienced.

---

3. Proactive circles are a type of restorative practice that are designed to establish the kinds of skills and climate that will build [effec- tive] communication and relationships, and will help minimize incidences of conflict

I wanted there to be a parallel just in case a student went home and talked about Circle and had parents freak out because they had no true understanding of it. And let me tell you, parent circles were the best! And it allowed the opportunity to create bonds that are usually not possible in traditional parent meetings. Parents felt empowered because, for some, they had a voice, even when they did not speak the same language. I'll never forget when one parent once said, "Circle makes me feel equal. Even though I do not read or write English or write and feel more comfortable speaking Spanish, in Circle, I am simply another parent wanting the same thing for my child. I can communicate in another way."

In my opinion, there are four types of proactive circles:
1.   Check-In/Check-out Circles (CICO)
2.   Community Building or Connecting Circles
3.   Dialogue or Topic Circles
4.   Academic Circles

Check-In/Out Circles

Check-in Circles are the simplest of the circles, but still vital to community building. Check-in circles are the best way to get a quick insight as to how your class is feeling, and it will ultimately build students' stamina to become familiar and more comfortable with the circle process. Such comfort and awareness will increase the desire to be a part of and take part in community-building circles-which last much longer than check-in circles.

Check-in circles tend to last between 5-12mins, depending on the number of participants. They do not go into depth or require expanded answers unless incited by the person speaking. They offer quick insights to the current mental, physical, or emotional state of your audience while allowing participants to practice how to successfully engage in the elements of circle such as using a talking piece and following the established guidelines.

Check-in circles, in my experience, are either undervalued or overused. I feel like Check-in circles are overlooked sometimes, or not seen as valuable. Some may feel there is no point in making time for such an activity that is only focusing on surface questions. But that could not be further from the truth. Those who understand the power of the Check-in will tell you that check-in circles are worth the time because you bear great fruit from planting such a small seed. The reward definitely is worth the time created. Students will begin to feel a connectedness to one another as well and the classroom environment, one that will reinforce their bonds and relationships.

Check-out circles are identical in format, except they happen at the end of the class or week. Sometimes you may even want to include a 'Check-up' circle, which happens on Wednesdays or whenever day or time you feel like it is necessary. When used consistently, these types of Circles can establish routine and ritual, which both are important in establishing expectations and creating a seamless culture.

Community-Building Circles

Surveys have shown that when people are asked what their worst fear is, it is not death. Death is actually second. The number one answer is public speaking. So, an amazing thing about circle is that it can potentially help with that fear and anxiety, while teaching interpersonal skills such as:

- Active listening
- Effective communication through speaking and listening
- Turn-taking
- Reflection on own experiences
- Empathy
- Compassion
- Mutual Support

On a deeper level, circles can help students create meaningful connections, learn similarities and differences, and build a strong foundation that will be helpful as the year progresses. Circles are rooted in the wisdom of Indigenous cultures, which adds to its significance as it allows the core beliefs and values of restorative thinking to take shape. The power of Circle is special as it honors an equal voice to all those participating and then creates mutual support and respect for one another. It allows students to bring parts of their lives into the classroom in an authentic way, which goes beyond the surface of just a designated calendar day or month. And if Circle occurs consistently, students will begin to carry the behaviors shown in Circle outside the classroom.

Dialogue or Topic Circles

This type of Circle allows for participants to discuss their thoughts and/or feelings about a particular topic or subject that has affected them. It is important to discuss current topics, particularly ones that may cause controversy or discomfort.

I remember the day after one of our most controversial elections. The 2016 election. And Trump had won. At the time, I was working as a Restorative Justice Teacher Advisor at a middle school in a very diverse, very prestigious Magnet in Glendale, California. Now I will admit, the overall consensus of the adults on campus was that Trump would NOT be the next president of the United States. So needless to say, we were very underprepared for the emotions and reactions of our students the very next day when in fact he won the presidency.

And just like how America has two sides of the aisle— our schools are sometimes set up in that same way, regardless of what you may think. And after two fights occurred at Nutrition, because of these opposing views, I knew that I had to do some- thing to allow our students to express their opinions without using their fists or harmful words.

. . . .

So, I quickly developed a Talking Circle script to give to teachers for their Advisories that day. And I also developed a lunchtime activity, that I titled 'Election Decompression.'

Now I would like for you to keep in mind that this happened in November, which means that students were already familiar with Circle, and had mostly developed a solid foundation and connection amongst each other. So, when I inquired with teachers later that week about how Circle went, those teachers who constantly incorporated Circle in their classes shared moments of connection and understanding. Whereas, those teachers who did Circle only once a month, experienced more difficulty with incorporating a safe space for students to share their perspectives.

And that's the key phrase right there... safe space. Students have to feel safe. Safe enough to know that their thoughts, feelings, and insights will be protected-REGARDLESS if it is popular opinion or not. Sharing your perspective and thoughts is a risk for anyone, student, or staff, and so those who choose to do so should feel like he or she will be heard and respected.

Academic Circles

Once students feel that sense of connectedness and safety, the academics will tend to come more naturally. Remember the title of this book: Humans First, Students Second.

. . . .

Circles focused on lessons or exams, or standardized testing (*eye roll) will also help students become more invested in their learning because a connection exists between something familiar and new information.

As a former English teacher, I know there are certain discussion strategies that exist that will prompt conversation but remember that Circle in this context is NOT that. This is not a Socratic Seminar or a Fishbowl. The Circle Process needs to still be implemented as well as all of its components: talking piece, guidelines, centerpiece, circle script.

Any teacher from any subject can use Academic Circles. Academic Circles can be used to access prior knowledge, introduce new information, or review for an exam. After each Unit, I used to have an Academic Reflection Circle for students to share how they personally connected to the material and how it may have affected them. I also allowed this time for them to offer feedback on how I could revise the Unit to make it that much better for the next set of students.

Circle Talk

In general, Circles are an incredible communication tool that also enhances participants' EQ (emotional intelligence). But let me say, that everything is NOT a Circle. Because, honestly, that's not practical. Life is complex and having a plethora of tools in your toolbox, so to speak, is how we learn to navigate all those twists and turns. But using Circle consistently, whether inside or outside the classroom, informal or formal, will have tremendous impact on daily life beyond communication, as it will build a sense of community and form strengthened relationships because students need a space to discuss issues unrelated to conflicts. Circles validate voices. Circles support choice. Circles show you care.

Show Your Authentic Self More August...

I remember the moment that the hiring freeze was finally over,   and I was finally able to sign a contract. Although I have always been able to make any class my own, whether I was a long-term sub or subbing for myself, the day had come where I finally would start the year and end the year as the teacher on record for a class that belonged exclusively to me-one that was genuinely and authentically mine. Interestingly enough, this also came in the year that the department decided that I would be a better fit as the 9th grade teacher (I had upper grades and AP at the time). As excited as I was to not have AP anymore- because that mess is *stressful* and some of the students, I felt were smarter than me lol- I was bummed to give up American Literature and Contemporary Composition as I felt like the content and teachings were growing me as a human in the same ways it was for my students. But since I was the person with least seniority and the one who could "handle" 9th grade (as proven from the position I was offered in the very beginning), I would become the ELA teacher for all 9th grade students.

At the time, I felt like I was about to have the worst years ever, being seen as just the "behavior person" who could handle "those kids"-which, by the way, is totally one of my trig- ger phrases (*insert angry emoji).

However, little did I know, I was about to embark on a completely new journey that would transform my life forever. Not only because of the educator that I became and still take pride in being, but also because of the people I shared a team with, who became my "teacher squad" and some of my closest friends until this very day. Not to mention, the students that I had the pleasure of guiding and leading, some of whom, are very much part of my life currently (gotta love social media). Plus, to top it off, I was able to create the best project-based curriculum plans and linked learning proj- ects ever written. The whole-child, holistic, trauma-informed, social justice restorative advocate was born.

In the first chapter, I suggested what you should do on those first few days of school and to NEVER, no matter what, start the very first day of school with your syllabus.

A statement that I feel very strongly about, however, I do know that you must go over your syllabus, before academic learning begins, so here is how I presented mine...

As I previously stated, those first few days are all about getting to know the students better and presenting "assignments", all focused on socio-emotional learning and/or community building, that will offer them a "cushion" of sorts as the semester progresses; this usually will keep the inherently unmotivated student participating at some level up until the very end almost. So, the day before I presented my syllabus, I would have students conduct a Quick Write (sometimes called Do Nows or Bell Work) in their Reader's/Writer's Notebook (RWNB or sometimes called an Interactive Notebook [INB]). I would ask each student to choose a poster in the room that they connected with-whether it be motivating, funny, confusing – just as long as it resonated with them in some way and tell me why they selected that poster.

This goes back to your room needing to be a welcoming space: full of bright colors, inspirational quotes and images, your own "all about you" teacher section, along with academic supports. I used to keep the 8 Parts of Speech, intended for elementary students, posted in the front of my room, because the grade level really doesn't mean anything when each student intellectually is on their own level. Studies have shown that our attention span only last about 8mins for adults, so imagine what a student's capacity is... therefore, you *have* to give them something worth looking at.

But back to the activity.

Once students completed the 'Do Now', I had them get up and move. (Sidenote: you have to have movement in your les- sons. A major piece of being culturally responsive and aware is to make sure you appeal to different learning styles through movement and engaging lessons). Each student had to move to the poster they selected. This afforded an organic community–building opportunity for students to see and make a connection to other students that they may not have even spoken to other- wise. When I had them move to their own areas of the room, I had them talk amongst each other before I asked for volunteers to share. This does two things:

1. Allows others to share in a safe space and
2. You are able to see who comfortable speaking whole class and those who shy away from it. This is crucial because having a variety of ways to acquire a response is also important in being a culturally responsive teacher.

After a few minutes, I use this moment to teach them the 'Call/Response' techniques that I enjoy using as a means to grab their attention. Being that Gwen Stefani's "Holla Back Girl" was a favorite of mine, my most commonly used Attention Signal is: 'When I Say Holla, You Say Back'. Some other favor- ites that can be used in any space are: 'When I say Are You, You say Ready', 'When I say I Need, You Say Quiet.'

I would then proceed in teaching them that I am going to repeat this phrase three times, and by the 3rd time, I expect stu- dents to have their attention focused on me which looks like eyes on me and sounds like silence (you also have to teach students these expectations-remember that they must be taught every-thing- from 4 to 14). So, I would then immediately give them the opportunity to practice this by instructing them to just start talking. After about 45 seconds, I say, "When I say holla, you say back. Holla....(back) Holla....(back) Holla...(back)."

Now if you believe that all the students met those expectations at 100%, you would be 100% incorrect. Being that this was their first time ever trying this, you have to expect that almost half of them will not be where you need them to be. So, this is an opportunity to not only show, and most importantly teach patience, as it starts to build the culture that not under- standing something on the first attempt is acceptable. That mis- takes and questions are acceptable. You don't always have to get it right on the first try.

I practice this about three more times before moving on, and by this point, about 80% know what I expect. But there will still be that 20% that will continue to say 'Hallelujah'. Or make sounds. Or say nothing at all. But that is normal and deemed proportionally acceptable within the tiered-pyramid of behavior. So, for those students you use gentle verbal reminders, in private, and do not make too much of a fuss about that particular behavior. You always want to pick and choose your battles and a proper Call/Response is not that major. But we will talk about responsive management and discipline that keeps and restores relationships in a later chapter.

After spending a day practicing the Attention Signal, and practicing effective communication skills, such as presenting orally and sharing ideas with peers, the very next day, I would go over the syllabus, but would preface it with my, what would soon become my famous, 'Drink the Water' speech.

Now before I continue, I must give credit where credit is due and the credit I must give for the title and concept of this beginning-of-the-year speech must go out to an amazingly talented, funny, and beautiful Science teacher from my alma mater. She also taught underclassmen and knew the importance of setting expectations within her classroom and having them adjust rather than they come in believing they would determine the tone. But she did this in such a real and authentic way that students formed immediate connections with her and wanted to make sure to uphold the classroom's ideals. Although I never had her as a teacher while I was a student, she was vital in sup- porting me those first couple years of my career. Moreover, of course, the most critical piece of my puzzle: her allowing me to use the phrase 'Drink the Water'.

So, on or around the third or fourth day of school, it is 'Drink the Water' speech day. A speech centered on reviewing the syllabus. So as students entered, I would have them get started on their 'Do Now', which was for them to respond to the following Aphorism: "You can lead a horse to water, but you cannot make them drink." (I would also have them write down the definition for 'aphorism' in the literary terms section of the back of their RWNB). So after about 5 minutes, I would ask for students to Turn-and-Talk to their neighbors and share their thoughts. Then I would ask for volunteers. I would explain and give other common examples of aphorisms they may be familiar with and then go ahead with my speech.

Now I cannot give you the speech verbatim, but the generic outline begins with me sharing some personal things about myself—where I grew up, what I was like in high school, and my 'Why'. The 'Why' is a vital part of anything that we do as a people because it reveals so much about the motivation and intention behind our actions. So, I would share all the reasons I was standing in front of them and why I would be forever apart of their life's journey, even after they were no longer in my class or even after they graduated from school. As soon as I was done offering personal tidbits about my life, I would pass out the syllabus to review.

By this point in my career, I knew how important it was that our classroom served as a safe space that felt like a team, or better yet, a family. So, from the very beginning, I began using the term 'Team 9' when speaking about anything that had to do with 9th grade as a collective. And at every moment I got, I would use the words 'family' or 'community'. Because just as the great Rita Pearson once said, "If you say things enough, they start to become a part of you." Therefore, I was very intentional about the language I used with my students, parents, colleagues, everyone. And later when I became grade level lead, our team wholeheartedly adopted the mindset of using the same language, which helped with continuity across the content areas as well as with building students' social-emotional skills. They heard the language of community and expectations throughout the day.

The syllabus was broken into the mandated necessary parts, but I most certainly did not read each section word-for-word and *please* make sure that you do not either. To ensure that students read it in its entirety, I would have a syllabus quiz a few days later-open syllabus if signed by their parent or guardian. So, we did more of a syllabus summary; I highlighted key points in each section and attached small anecdotes to them—a little trick that I learned from another amazingly awesome educator. She had such a profound impact on my decision to become a teacher.

To begin with, when I had her as a student initially in the 11th grade for an elective, I begged my counselor to let me have her again as a senior for Government even though she taught "general education" and I was in "the Magnet". She became someone that I trusted and depended on; I felt completely safe with her. I remember when 9/11 happened, her room was the first one I went to and stayed in all day as the nation was trying to process what had just occurred. She went beyond the class- room and District-mandated lessons; she helped her students see her as a real human being. Moreover, she continued to be that real human each and every day. Even after I graduated, she supported me during my first couple of years of teaching at my alma mater and supported me as a new mother too, arranging play dates for our kids. She influenced the shape of the type of teacher I wanted to be. One who was compassionate, funny, and cared authentically about her students.

Keeping her in mind, I would discuss each section of the syllabus by sharing a relevant story. My intentions were to have them know that high school was a fresh start, a clean slate. That who they were last year, or even yesterday, or sometimes before walking into our classroom, that none of that mattered if they wanted to make the changes necessary to be better. I would tell them that who their family was, or the generational patterns did not matter—this was their time to start anew. Mentioning this would always get their attention. Because, you see, if no one ever showed you a different way or a different perspective, you begin to believe there is only one way or option. Our job as educators is to present our students with multiple ways to achieve success and break patterns and choose their own path.

So, I would talk about how I didn't care if they failed every single class prior to that moment. Or that no one in his or her family made it through the 10th grade. Or if they were only there at school because they had to be by law. Or if they were there because they were determined to uphold their perfect attendance or dreams of becoming valedictorian. Whatever the reason, I wanted to empower each of my students and let each of them know that I would be there to support them along the journey, every step of the way, through every bumpy obstacle, until we reached the water. And standing at the water's edge, we would discuss what the water represented to them personally: knowledge, success, growth, compassion, empathy, forgiveness, a new understanding, perseverance, or resiliency. Then I would remain quiet, while standing there with them, and wait—until they were ready to drink and continue on their journey.

Thus the 'Drink the Water' speech.

I made sure that I demonstrated fully to my students that I would be there for them through it all. Because my goal was to make them better humans. But as much as I, or anyone else in their universe, wanted that for them, I could lead the horse to water, but could not make it drink. Therefore, the mantra 'Drink the Water' became words to live by it. And many of my babies continue to live until this very day. I have former students who will still contact me and say, "I'm drinking the water, Ms. Hardy." And it leaves me with more words the amaz- ing Rita Pearson said about legacy and the power that lives in the relationships we create and the mark that we leave on the world.

Shared Experience Moment

- Who was the person or persons that influenced you to be the type of educator that you are today?

- What legacy would you like to leave behind?

- What would you include in your own 'Drink the Water' speech?

Restorative Recipe #3
Recognize that Words Have Power

—

Another critical part of creating a restorative community and making those proper shifts to a more restorative way of living is based in the language that we use. To speak restoratively takes practice and intention. You have to make sure that the implications and tones behind words spoken are all rooted in strengthening the community by upholding two of the 5 R's of Restorative: Respect and Relationships. Our language can either uplift social-emotional health and development or it can tear it all down. Words matter and can have lasting effects.

Many of us come from the generation where you are to respect your elders regardless of how they speak or make you feel. Where kids are to be seen and not heard. Where the reasons for actions do not matter and punishment was usually harsh and unrelated to the inappropriate behavior. Where blame and shame were the goal. This type of discipline affects the person who experienced it and will also influence the way discipline is implemented in all areas of life. So, as an educator, you must be mindful of this while shifting your mindset and building your climate and culture.

Because this generation is set up differently. And rightfully so. Yes, countless cultural traditions and beliefs have been traditions and beliefs for generations. Nevertheless, it is up to us now to break those generational cycles packed with toxicity; and it can start with the language we use. This is a simple and effective approach that each one of us has individual choice and control over. So restorative language should be used throughout the building, classrooms, and common spaces. Because if everyone plays their part, a community focused on relationships, responsibility, and accountability will blossom and eventually flourish.

On the Restorative Practices Continuum, affective statements are an informal practice that can be used within all Tiers of the MTSS-model. Affective statements, sometimes known as 'I' statements, are statements that connect personal emotions to the actions of others. Affective statements help someone express to another person how their behavior affected others, whether that be positive or negative. How many times has the phrase, 'I never knew you felt that way' or the question of, 'Why didn't you tell me?' ever come up for you once conflict occurred? That is probably because several of us struggle to express our feelings in a healthy way.

In education, we, too commonly and quickly, scold or yell at students when misbehavior occurs. If we took the time to identify our feelings, however, such behavior may not occur again.

I remember one year I was out at a conference for 3 days and so I needed a guest teacher while I was away. (Notice how I used 'guest teacher' and not substitute). Now my expectation for my students was that they were to treat a guest teacher even better than they treated me and that I expected them to show the guest teacher what Team9 stood for and to represent me properly. Well, needless to say, the classes as a collective fell short of my expectations. So when I returned, and read the note that was left, and checked the incentive chart for great moments, I was beyond disappointed, bordering angry, and most certainly embarrassed.

But I did not yell nor lecture them on their behavior. Instead, I simply said, "I am so deeply disappointed and embarrassed with the overall behavior all of you showed our guest when I was away. According to this note, Team9 did not shine in the ways I am used to- did not show up in the ways I am used to- and for that, I feel hurt. What I need right now is for you to reflect on your behavior the past 3 days and remain in silence for the rest of the period. We will sit in Circle and discuss this further at a later time."

When I tell you that by the end of the class, I had students handing me apology notes and letters and wanting to talk after- school, I knew that our foundation as a class was solid- that our actions and emotions were linked to the relationships we had with one another. Not rules. Not fear. But relationships. And when we had our

Circle later that week, I was not the teacher, but a member of the Team 9 community who wanted to discuss how we felt about the behaviors of some of our fellow teammates so that we could collaboratively develop some agreements for the next time I needed to be away. Having the entire class involved in the discussion means I also had them apart of the solution, and because of this just like the

Respect Agreement' or Classroom Expectations they are more inclined to make sure everyone is responsible for upholding the solution. And the next time I was out they were vastly different.

The use of affective statements shifts from blame and accusations, to ownership over personal feelings and emotions. It makes available the vocabulary to explain needs and name feelings. And by using a label (Team9), students are challenged to rise to the expectations and characteristics of what that means. I, too, am also separating the students from their actions, which also reiterates I know them beyond this one incident. School may be the only place where this skill can be introduced, practiced, and developed.

EQ (emotional intelligence) is just as important, if not more important, as IQ.

So, I suggest having a 'word wall' with emotion stem starters and feeling words. The sentence frame that I like most comes from the *Restorative Resources* practice sheet which goes as follows:

Humans 1st Students 2nd

....

I feel _____ (state the impact/emotion)
When_____(identify the behavior or event)
Because _____ (reason for the emotion).

If you would like to take it a step further, you can add the sentence:

What I would like is_____(state the desired behavior)[4]

With the 'Sub' story I used earlier, I could have used the above sentence frame like this:
I feel disappointed when I go away and learn that my students were not showing up as their best selves to class because I see the best parts of each of you daily. What I would like is for you to treat any guest in this classroom better than you treat me, especially when I am not present. Affective statements, although the least formal restorative practice on the continuum, provide insight to feelings, establish expectations as well as boundaries, encourage personal accountability, and build empathy and connection. Affective statements are also a way for everyone to practice sharing their feelings which in turn will begin to normalize emotion.

---

[4] Affective Statement Practice. https://www.restorativeresources.org/uploads/5/6/1/4/56143033/affective_statements_practice.pdf

....

With the continual use of affective statements, the stigmas associated with feelings will, hopefully, begin to fade with the safety of Circle and thus become part of everyday life. Eventually, everyone will internalize the feelings one has belong to that person and is their truth. And no one can tell someone else about those feelings. There is no "right or wrong" or "good or bad". All feelings can take up space, without judgment, and serve a purpose.

R-E-S-P-E-C-T Me
Early September

—

When you walk into most classrooms, you will see a poster on the wall that determines the 'Classroom Rules'. Sadly, most are these are store bought which means no real connection exists between that poster and your classroom. And even if you write the 'rules' in your own language, by yourself, that still eliminates the most important group- your students-from being a part of its construction, which means there still will be no real connection to that poster, which also means that you will prob- ably be spending a great deal of time reprimanding students for not following the rules on that poster.

Therefore, in order to avoid this from occurring, you must engage students in the process of creating 'Classroom Expectations'. Now you may have noticed that I did not say "rules" and that is very intentional. First, I do not like that word as it carries negative connotations with it, just as the word "discipline", but that is another story. The word 'Rules' also implies that you have power control over others, which if you remember from the Social Discipline Window of the first chapter, your goal should be not to control and use power over, but to guide and use power with. So, with that in mind, drop rules from your vocabulary and replace it with expectations as the effect on a person may impact them differently when you say:

"Here are the expectations that we as a class community are going to hold each other to"

Versus

"Here are the rules that you need to obey while in class"

In my role as an out-of-classroom support personnel, I remember this one class of 4th graders that I had known from the time they were in the 1st grade. As with many elementary school schedules, a certain class or pod of students typically stay together for almost the entire duration of their elementary career. This can be either genius or disastrous. And coming from a teacher who knows what it is like to have one class out of my six that earned the label "that one class", I knew what the teachers of this group were feeling and dealing with. Because typically, the students in "that one class" struggled with displaying their best selves when it came to one another, teacher included. And even though there were a multitude of circum- stances out of their control that influenced their behavior over the years- teacher turnover, non-credentialed teachers, first-year teachers, long-term subs, split classes, students moving in and out- these students had spent enough time with one another, and with me, to know to do better. But they just needed a little bit more guidance and support...

"Ms. Hardy we have some concerns about that one 4th grade class," remarked the Assistant Principal at our weekly check- in, "so I would like for you to go in and conduct not only an observation, but to also do a Respect Agreement[5] lesson with them."

Being that I had knowledge of the dynamics of the classroom, I knew that students in this class needed two things: 1. Constant Engagement with no Downtime and 2. A Structured Way to Communicate.

I had done plenty of Respect Agreements (Figure 2) with my own students as well as other classes and groups, but I knew, for this class, that I needed to adjust the lesson a little in order to ensure maximum effectiveness. What I did with my high school students probably would not have the same bearing with elementary school students, especially those who were already having a hard time with showing up as their best selves.

With this in mind, I decided to modify the steps to creating a Respect Agreement by:

- Breaking the quadrants into multiple days, so that the time spent on creating this agreement was meaningful and given their full attention
- Creating a worksheet that had my questions on them already so that students had time to write their thoughts before sharing them whole group
- Intentionally grouping the students so that I could prevent potential conflict amongst certain students
- Assigning roles within those groups

- Using a discussion protocol that allowed for all voices to be heard, but when sharing whole group, had only the designated person from each group speak out

In a restorative community, one way to confirm expectations amongst any group, whether it be for a classroom or staff meeting, is creating a Respect Agreement.

*Complete lesson plan on my website

Shared Experience Moment

- What are some key behaviors you find essential to classroom expectations?

- What does RESPECT look like to you? Sound like to you?

- At this very moment, on a scale to 1 to 5, 1 being super skeptical and 5 being total believer, how successful do you believe a Respect Agreement could be?

---

5 A Respect Agreement is a collaborative 'living' document created primarily by students under the guidance of the educator. It is a set of expectations that all members of the classroom community agree to follow

Restorative Recipe #4
R-E-S-P-E-C-T

—

In my trials of discovering who I was as an educator in the first few chapters, I learned that moving out of the 'Permissive' box meant that I needed to not only have my kids have amazing relationships with me, but I also needed each one of them to respect me in a genuine way. This only came with not only extending them respect, regardless of their age, but also to set transparent boundaries, clear expectations, and high levels of support. This is part of the process of setting up a culture of authenticity because students know when they are truly respected and cared for versus being disliked and/or tolerated.

Such a concept is usually lost in school systems. Traditionally in our school systems, but particularly in elementary schools, I noticed that fear-based models are usually the go-to discipline system. "I am going to call your mother", "I'm going to get such and such", "I'm going to take away your recess for the rest of the week." There are a few issues with such threats:

1. The follow-through of the threat may not occur or be feasible.
2. The overuse of the threat makes the threat no longer powerful and eventually useless.

3. Students will not change their behavior permanently, only when authority figures are present.

4. Indirectly teaches students that their behavior should only be different after being threatened with some sort of punishment.

The bottom-line is threats and punishments are only short- term fixes. And since we have already established that behavior can only change from within, and that change occurs through our connections with one another, as educators we should strive to not set strict rules that students must obey, but instead establish a Respect Agreement which states how each person within that setting is expected to treat one another. And the key ingredient to this is to then TEACH the agreed upon behaviors so that everyone knows what to do because students generally do not know how to be successful independently. The idea is to create opportunities and spaces to engage with your students, not try to control or manage them. Providing students choice and voice will help rein- force positive behaviors as well as praising and/or acknowledging the behaviors that contribute positively to the environment.

Figure 2: Respect Agreement

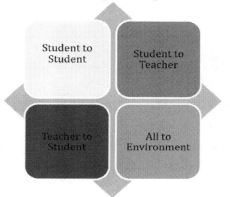

Respect Agreements are broken into 4 quadrants. Each quadrant emphasizes the relationship between certain groups. This agreement establishes the expectations in a specific setting. Every member of the setting takes part in its creation. The groups can be changed according to the audience.

Respect agreements are a collaborative creation between all those included in a setting to hold everyone accountable for their behaviors. It is a way to establish norms and values for the classroom, or other setting, throughout the school year. This could be teacher and students. Administrator and faculty. Coach and team. Lead teacher and colleagues. Its key purpose is to ensure that everyone's voice is heard. After a consensus is reached, the Respect Agreement is then posted in a visible and prominent area- I would have each student sign it as well as myself. And if and when conflict arrives, the Respect Agreement serves as an aide to redirect and discuss inappropriate behaviors. Ask the question: 'How does what's happening here fit with our Agreements?' It promotes a common language and a set of behaviors that equate respect, which in turn promotes the values of teamwork and unity. Something extremely important in promoting a positive culture; in establishing community.

Respect Agreements may not be on the continuum of Restorative Practices, but it is most certainly an intricate part of any restorative community.

How Strong is Your Foundation?
October

—

By this time of the year, you are probably feeling pretty confident and happy. The year may seem to be floating by; but as with good things, they sometimes come to an end-or at least take a detour. This is what I believe mid-October through
November to be.

Since I am from California, I compare this time of year to an earthquake. You never know if and when the "big one" is going to come and dismantle all that you have built. Or maybe there is a shaker that knocks some foundational screws loose and minor repairs are needed. Sometimes you may have a slow- roller, where you can just ride it out without even getting out of bed. Or you may have small tremors that you barely feel, but may have you questioning yourself, like, "Was that just an earthquake? Or am I tripping?" Regardless of the magnitude, earthquakes can cause damage to property, similar to how conflict or inappropriate behavior can cause damage to relation- ships. Therefore, regardless of the assumed magnitude, damage needs assessment so that the proper attention can be given to repair or restore the harm that has occurred.

If you have been truly intentional about building

community within your classroom, behavior disruptions or conflicts have probably been at a minimum, but don't ever think that inappropriate behaviors will disappear completely. As students learn and grow, mistakes and all the inappropriate behaviors that come with it will occur. However, if minimal conflict has not been the case and chaos seem to still be occurring on a daily basis, then return to the previous chapters and start reviewing your entire Tier I systems, routines, and practices.

Mid-first semester is a funny time in the school year. It is at this point where students and teachers are both looking for- ward to breaks and where, sadly, students are traditionally broken into two groups: those on track to pass and those who are not. And so, for those students who are not, the desire to remain academically invested can quickly fade away.

Side note: this is exactly why I adopted a "no-zero" grading policy, used a weighted scale for grades, allowed retakes of major assignments, and accepted late work up until a deadline, which was usually two weeks prior to the end of the final grading period. On a traditional 100-point scale, zeros significantly affect a student's grade in ways that may seem an impossible feat to overcome. Trust me, you do not want this type of mindset or energy sitting in your classroom for how many weeks or months even. It's demoralizing to students when they feel as if there is no chance of succeeding. Therefore, you want students to feel as if success is attainable, as long as they put in some effort.

'So you're telling me to just give grades for effort?' 'Yes and No.'

You have to ask yourself this question: what is your ultimate goal for your students? Ideally, we want all of our students to absorb every single morsel of knowledge we feed them- to "Drink the Water". But the reality of the situation is not every kid is thirsty. And some don't like water- they like tea. Or soda. Or coffee. Or beverages they have no business drinking right now. What do we do then? As educators, what do we do?

We must meet students where they are. Then build from there.

My goal was that my students do the work I assigned them- and I never wanted to rob them of that opportunity. Yes, I understand that a no-late work policy promotes responsibility, organization, and meeting deadlines. Yes, I get that. But we do not have to teach every single lesson in the long lists of lessons to ever exist in the book of life lessons all at once in our class- room in every situation. Instead, we should focus on what our students need; and at the top of that list, I am always going to advocate for grace, compassion, and understanding. And for them to keep striving towards understanding content until they get it.

So instead of giving a 'o' for an assignment, with no chance of redemption, I would simply mark it as 'missing'. During Advisory, each student would have a weekly assignment check to bring awareness and conversation to their current aca- demic standing. After school, I would set my tutoring hours the same time each week (mirroring college professors while setting my own boundaries) and throughout the week, I would place sticky-notes on students' desk that read: "I hope I see you today/tomorrow/" or "I missed you yesterday at tutoring". I also made sure after each unit, students knew that we would be building on some of the same skills and concepts, so that it was very much possible to improve grades, if that is what they needed. Lastly, I did not take it personally if a student did not do a homework assignment, revel in the amazement of my lesson, or even remember it for that matter. And again, I ask, honestly, when was the last time you used the Pythagorean Theorem in a real-life situation? (My apologies Math Gurus...) Point is, focus on the skills that really matter for that student and for some, it's not academic, but interpersonal. Adopting these practices supported the student holistically while still upholding the high expectations I had. Because, to be clear, "the concept of high expectations does not mean no mistakes, no second chances, or moving fast. It means:

- Doing challenging things
- Doing challenging things until getting them right
- Working hard
- Asking for help[6]

Ok... back to my original purpose for this chapter... October is the time for inappropriate behaviors to rock the Richter scale for sure. For this reason, I hope a strong foundation of solid relationships and connections between students and their peers, and teachers and their students have already been established because *you cannot repair or restore a relationship that does not exist.* Please highlight, write down, make a poster, underline, or just do whatever you need to in order to remember that above-mentioned italicized statement. It is a super important concept to understand. Since the most critical function of restorative practices is building and restoring relationships, relationships have to first exist between individuals. Otherwise, a restorative approach will probably be ineffective.

I remember an October when I was not at all that restorative in my approaches because I had it up to the ceiling with students coming in tardy. Student tardiness is most definitely one of my triggers, my buttons, my pet peeves. I had a wall, near the door, that read, 'Ms. Hardy's Not so Fun Tardy Party'. As was the established protocol, students were to enter the room, quietly, without interruption or noise, with their tardy slip and tape it to the wall. If they had more than one, then they would place it on top of the one(s) already there.

---

6 Maynard N. and Weinstein B. 102. *Hacking School Discipline 9 Ways to Create a Culture of Empathy & Responsibility and Using Restorative Justice.* 2020. Highland Heights, OH. Times Ten Publication.

The first one was a Warning; but the second one and any others that followed were time owed, because I felt like if you decide to take away from my time, I most certainly was going to take away from yours. It went from 5 mins, to 10mins, to 20mins, to 30mins, to an hour. But once students came and "served their time"- which is a criminalizing and punitive phrase now that I think about it- they were able to rip up their tardy slips and throw them away, and the process restarted if necessary. This again is so that students feel like they have an opportunity for redemption; that their past choices will not be held against them for the rest of eternity, especially after they have made amends.

Well one day, one of my students came in late, and not only was she late, she came in with Starbucks and a Boba for her friend. Maybe I subconsciously desired a breakfast beverage; because I became so enraged that this young lady had the audacity to come into my room tardy, again, but yet found the time to stop for treats.

So, as she started to walk to her desk, I stopped what I was doing (which was direct instruction at the time) and focused all of my energy, which also inadvertently redirected the entire class's energy as well, on her.

"Well, it is so nice for you to join us," I said sarcastically. "And I see you were being so thoughtful to your friend, but apparently have no consideration for your other classmates or me, since now I am stopping all that, I am doing to speak to you-who has come to class late. Again."

She stood with her hip popped to one side and blankly stared at me, which made me even more upset. So, in a split, not-so- smart decision (hindsight 20/20), I went over to her desk, picked it up (literally), stormed out the classroom door, and put the desk, in the hallway, facing the wall.

"Since you seem to have no regard for this class nor time, you can sit outside. Because right now, you're taking up space and air of those who actually want to be here." I know. Horrible. Smh... Definitely not one of my great teaching moments.

She scoffed and said, "Whatever, Hardy," and walked outside to sit in the seat. And while I was trying to shame her by having her isolated outside and make her feel guilty for not caring for the class, the opposite effect took place. Sitting outside, she was able to enjoy her beverage, not do any of my class- work, and talk to whoever passed by. She was living the dream. And due to my actions, her and I's relationship suffered some major damage. I reacted instead of responding. There is a major difference.

Shared Experience Moment

- What are your classroom triggers or triggers in general?

- Have you ever gotten so mad at a student or colleague that you reacted before fully thinking things through?

- How would you have handled my Starbucks/Boba moment?

Restorative Recipe #5 Stop. Think. Respond. Restore.

—

Restorative practices are rooted in positive relationships – especially between students and adults. Similar to how students who know their peers better will more than likely be better to each other, the same logic exists between students and adults. It is less likely that a student will disrespect or act defiantly towards an adult he or she has a positive relationship with and knows genuinely cares. John C. Maxwell emphasizes this point when he said, "Students don't care how much you know until they know how much you care."

If I were asked how I would classify my teaching style, I would never mention the word 'disciplinarian' because that type of firm, rigid, authoritarian style was not true to me, which is something that I learned in those first couple of years of my teaching career. I really had to find my balance. And once I began trusting in and becoming restorative in my ways, my students and I both flourished. It wasn't the rules that kept our classroom together, but the relationships and expectations we had with one another.

Now the anecdote I just shared for this chapter definitely was not a reflection of the general sense of community and connectedness my classes shared with one another. But I am human, and humans (young and not-so-young) have their moments where they react. In my anger and frustration, I resorted back to the "traditional" soil that I grew up in and witnessed in my days of coaching other teachers. The need to assert my authority as well as inflict some sort of punishment that would invoke shame in my student so that she would not repeat that behavior was my goal. In elementary school, this may look like students standing along the wall during recess or sitting in the corner. In secondary school, it could be my example or some other form of exclusionary measure such as keeping students from a preferred activity or sending them out of the classroom to the office.

Let me be clear: I am not saying that teachers who do this or have done this are horrible teachers. I just believe that they have rooted themselves in that 'traditional' punitive soil that emphasizes punishment and exclusionary measures as an effective way of influencing behavior. When in reality, using those types of practices only causes resentment and anger between student and teacher, especially if the student feels the reaction was unfair.

What to do in that moment?

Have a Restorative Chat using Restorative (Affective) Questions.

Restorative chats are the next step of action on our Restorative Practices Continuum (see Figure 3). This continuum shows the range of actions that someone can take to remain restorative throughout any interaction. From left to right, it moves from informal to formal practices. The more formal the practice, the more planning, time, structure, and usually people, it takes in order to be as effective and impactful as possible. Each practice builds on basic communication skills as well, adding elements to address the increased complexity: conflicts, harms, power imbalances, and multiple participants. The goal of these practices is to take situations where punitive actions, such as sending a student to the office, are replaced with ways to teach the student how to repair harm, rebuild relationships, and reintegrate smoothly. You know that your school or work community is truly restorative when 80% of your interactions with others are more informal. Such an indication exhibits a strong foundation rooted in relationships and connections.

Figure 3: Restorative Practices Continuum

Source: Costello (2010)

Restorative chats are the first types of responsive actions one can take once some type of violation or harm occurs. This type of conversation is not intended for situations where one or more persons has caused significant harm-that would require a more formal circle which we will discuss in a later chapter. This type of chat should last no longer than 10 minutes. But just remember, while these chats are fairly quick in nature, they may take quite a bit of practice to fully master.

Restorative chats have restorative questions, also known as affective questions, one can use to engage the individual in conversation that focuses on the feelings surrounding an incident. The idea is to address an immediate issue and have the person(s) reflect on their behavior. Using Restorative Questions for low- level incidents can also prevent a larger event from occurring later.

There is a general flow to Restorative Questions. Traditionally, they are the same five questions, but the following will offer some variety so that you do not come off sounding super robotic and/or rehearsed. This is how I would ask the "traditional" restorative questions when speaking to a student:

1. Can you tell me what happened, step-by-step?
2. What were you thinking about at the time? How did you feel?
3. Who has been affected by what you did? How are they affected?
4. How do you feel now about what happened?
5. What needs to happen now to make things as right as possible?
6. In the future, if something similar is happening, what can you do differently?

The first question is vital in creating a sense of fairness since the individual will be able to explain the event in his or her or their own words. It is critical not to interrupt nor influence the narrative being expressed in order for true reflection and ultimately, hopefully, improved behavior and decision- making. It takes a skillful approach and established climate of trust in order to help an individual accept responsibility for his or her actions and to manage the feelings that may accompany that acknowledgement. Those five questions are also just as vital as the first since both promote reflection and conflict resolution. I have had students decide to make posters or sing a song as forms of apology to their classmates or me. And once you know how a person would like to improve his or her own behavior, it helps to make a plan for when and if conflict occurs. This becomes especially powerful because it allows for the individual to have input, which transforms into ownership, over choices and behaviors.

Nervous about not being to memorize all the questions? No worries. These Restorative Questions can be put on wallet- sized cards to fit in your pocket, or attach to your lanyard, or to go in a plastic holder for your ID-which is what I did for all my staff and faculty. Remember to also present a neutral or concerned facial expression matched with a lower tone of voice and language neutrality. Make sure to take a deep breath before speaking to ground yourself as well, because many times our reactions, even when attempting to diffuse a situation, can, in fact, escalate it because our own emotions get in the way.

However, sometimes, despite the most skilled facilitator, some people are not ready yet to own up to their misdoings and poor choices- especially our younger babies who know lying can usually keep them out of trouble. That is why it is crucial to have already established a positive relationship, so that the likelihood of lying or lack of ownership decreases.

Even still, there will be times when, regardless of the relationship you have with someone, that person may not be ready to deal with the consequences of admitting involvement or ownership of misbehavior. There have been numerous times where students have looked me in my eye and lied about their behavior choices- but there are consequences that come with that. So, if you find yourself speaking to someone that does not seem ready or willing to take accountability for his or her actions, then a Restorative Chat may not be the appropriate action to take. A more formal, or traditional, approach may need to be taken.

'Tis the Season
November/December

—

By this point in the year, a lot of both students and teachers   are ready for the time off that occurs in November and December. As a result, short tempers and low tolerance are possibilities. Therefore, these months can naturally give an opportunity for any community to practice one of the many extremely important socio-emotional traits that are key to this work, and most importantly, to one's humanity: Empathy.

I will never forget this one circle that I had with one class of my ninth graders.

We were actually conducting an Academic Circle, discussing character analysis. In attempts to have students connect with what they were reading, I wanted them to either recall a time when they had personally struggled with something or share a time when they saw someone struggle with something.

Just a quick reminder that when you are in Circle, responses are voluntary. By simply sitting within Circle and listening to others, means active participation in the process. There should never be a 'pass maximum' (which I have observed). Maintaining a choice to pass also helps to build trust in the process and honor each other's truth and choice. However, Circle can only be as effective as those sitting within it, so courageous participants are vital as well. Thus, when anyone speaks and shares his or her or their experiences, I always feel a sense of pride because that means he or she feels safe enough to do so. And so there might be times when I ask that each participant speak, like for introductions of their name, but then I promise them that if they don't want to speak again after that, they do not have to. All students will not push back on this involuntary response, and it gives you the first opportunity to build more trust in Circle by not forcing verbal participation after that.

If you find that many students are passing (as is the case sometimes in the first couple of Circles), then you should reevaluate the topic or ask students to supply questions/topics they would like to discuss. Sometimes to elicit responses, I pass the Talking Piece around a couple of times until I get at least 5-7 responses out of a group of 20-25.

Okay, back to the story...Now mind you, when I first thought of these Circle Questions, I figured the responses were going to be surface, but I was pleasantly surprised when one student had the courage to share something extremely personal, which then incited an overwhelming response of concern, connection, and of course, empathy.

As the Talking Piece[7] - which happened to be a paper shoe to connect to the idea of walking in someone else's shoes (complete Circle Script available on the website)- was going around the Circle, stopping every 2 students or so, I glanced across the Circle, observing one student in particular who seemed extremely nervous. He was bouncing his leg vigorously and rocking back and forth, eyes staring toward the Centerpiece.[8] He looked up briefly to watch how close the Talking Piece was to him- which was only about 4 students away. Suddenly, I began to notice his chest moving methodically up and down, so as to keep deep breaths. Then the Talking Piece was in his hands. He gazed down towards the paper shoe, rotating it between his fingers for about 45 seconds.

I could sense everything he was feeling without him saying a word as body language is a critical part of non-verbal communication. And as you may know, non-verbal communication is how we humans primarily communicate our thoughts and emotions.

Another Sidenote: Early on, at the beginning of holding Circle, participants were told that it was okay to hold the Talking Piece for a moment before speaking to gather thoughts and/or to build the courage to speak. Everyone else in the Circle was to give the one holding the Talking Piece the time and space he or she needed. And honestly, silence is a way of communicating too. As he continued to spin the shoe, he kept taking deep breaths and then he stopped, looked up at me, then his best friend, then began to speak.

---

7 A Talking Piece is an object that is used within Circle to show who is the designated speaker at the time. Talking Pieces should be significant to the Circle and serve as an equalizer providing opportunity for any participant to contribute their thoughts and feelings.

He shared a time when he struggled with something and that something was him being bullied for 2 years in middle school. He then went on to share the details of one particular incident that took place after school on a playground that really caused trauma and pain both physically and mentally.

As he shared details of being punched in the face, shoved to the ground, and kicked repeatedly in the back, the room fell eerily silent as others were processing what they were hearing. And then suddenly, I began to hear sniffles and saw heads bowed or eyes glued on the speaker.

Then suddenly, the young man speaking jumped up out of his seat and ran towards the door- tears vividly streaming down his face. The room gasped collectively as we watched him leave, feeling every ounce of his pain. Two of his closest friends ran after him. I looked around at faces unfamiliar to this contrast of the usual happiness and cheerfulness that was our classroom. I knew that I needed to do something. "I know what was just shared was super heavy," I said to them. "But I want you all to know that I am thankful for how all of you are respecting the speaker and honoring his experiences.

---

8 A Centerpiece is a collection of items significant to the Circle Keeper and/or the group of participants. It should always include the guide- lines and possibly the values shared by the group

I'm sure that it was not easy for him to share and possibly relive that past trauma, but I commend all of you for making him and anyone else that may have experienced something similar feel safe." I paused for a few moments, before considering my next words.

"I am going to pass the talking piece around the circle again, and if you feel like allowing your heart to guide you and you would like to share what you are feeling, then please do so."

One by one, students began to share how they either could relate to a similar experience or how they had no idea that someone who was happy and well-liked suffered such pain or that hurting someone else in the attempts to be cool in front others was just plain stupid and cruel.

We were just about at the last person sharing when the door opened and the students who had left walked in. And to my surprise, students within the Circle began to get up, walk over, and meet that one student with hugs and pats on the shoulders or words of encouragement and support.

I was amazed. And even now, as I type this story, I have tears in my eyes, yet a smile on my face because I was able to witness a moment of authentic human connection. A moment that I never knew was going to happen but did happen because of the classroom environment we had established. And it was beautiful.

Shared Experience Moment

Think of a time when you witnessed empathy amongst your students?

- What actions were taken, or words being spoken?
- How did that change the relationships / dynamics amongst those persons?
- What circumstances led up to that moment?
- How did you this experience help you grow and in what ways?

Restorative Recipe #6
Walk in Someone Else's Shoes

—

Restorative practices are rooted in positive relationships – especially between students and adults. Similar to how students who know their peers better will more than likely be less rude, mean, or disrespectful, students who feel connected in a positive way are more than likely willing to consider and view different perspectives. The beauty, the magic, and the power of Circle is that care and support show up in ways of sympathy, listening, words of affirmation, hugs, and one of the most important emotional and life skills to have: empathy.

In the story I just shared, students who may not have known more than each other's name were now hugging, crying, or simply, holding a safe space for emotions to freely flow. This is why Circle, initially, can be mistaken for therapy. But let me be clear, that Circle is not therapy (even if it feels therapeutic) and you as the adult are not required to offer advice to "fix" or "heal" the student- this is what empathy is not. One way to ensure this does not occur is to ask the question that a former supervisor once asked me: Do you want me to simply listen so you can vent, or would you like my advice?

I was actually taken aback by the question because it had never been asked of me before. And yet, it was the type of question I had been missing all my life. And from that moment, it is now a question that I now ask of others to hopefully evoke the same feelings I immediately had. I really believe that it is a communication game-changer. Because you then learn to listen without interruption, or minimization, and respect the wishes of the speaker. If something traumatic is shared, however, you can find outside support and help that student get the proper support he or she needs.

One of the best definitions of empathy I have come across is from a scientific journal about social neuroscience. The two authors, Decety and Lamm (2006: 1146) define empathy as the capacity to recognize the emotion that another person is experiencing. It is the ability to understand and not confuse those feelings between oneself and others. This distinction provides someone with the opportunity to connect with an event or emotion outside of their own personal experiences which then can lead to other feelings such as compassion and understanding. This is something we can relate to as we sometimes play the "therapist" for our students.

Although this book focuses primarily on restorative approaches, a vital element of setting up a strong school or work culture is to also incorporate social-emotional learning (SEL). Explicitly teaching how to recognize, regulate, and respond to emotions is key and, honestly, directly linked to academic success. The Collaborative for Academic, Social, and Emotional Learning (CASEL) outlines the following five social and emotional components necessary for elementary and middle school students and recommends that all schools incorporate each of them within their curriculums and/or programs:

a. Self-awareness

b. Self-management

c. Social Awareness

d. Relationship Skills

e. Responsible decision-making[9]

In order to build and sustain healthy relationships rooted in common values, students, as well as adults, need SEL lessons and activities. And I know how this may pose difficulty because there is only so much time in the school day. And, of course, we know that not just one lesson or Circle will change someone's habits, behavior, or mindset. However, SEL and character building are just as important as academics, if not more. We wouldn't leave the acquirement of reading and math skills to chance, would we? Not at all. So why would we not be intentional about developing emotional and social skills? Just think about all of the super intelligent jerks walking around-they may have the book smarts, but emotional intelligence is key.

Howard Zehr, known as the godfather of restorative justice (RJ), while describing its foundations, states that engaging with RJ requires that we examine and change the lenses through which we see the world.[10] How we view the world comes from our perspective, which is shaped by our experiences. A number of individuals can experience the same event, yet their perspectives may differ. Our perspectives come from our beliefs and values. All of these together impact our decisions and actions.

The Little Book of Restorative Justice in Education does a great job of explaining this impact further. It uses an eyeglasses metaphor. It explains that beliefs are specific ideas that one believes to be fact, even though it cannot be fully proven. Our beliefs come from feelings, trust, and conviction, despite the fact they are rooted in intuition, upbringing, sociocultural contexts, or personal experience. However, beliefs are a key piece to how we see the world as they are the frames of our glasses. These frames are the framework, the mindset, the perspective that guides how each of us decide to live.[11] And whether or not we choose to acknowledge it, our personal beliefs one hundred percent impact our classrooms and how we interact with students, parents, colleagues, administration, and the community. For example, if you believe that black and brown students who live in "the hood" are incapable of learning complex ideas or producing exceptional work by thinking outside of the box, then you might "dumb down" your curriculum, not recommend many for AP

---

9 What is the CASEL Framework? https://casel.org/fundamentals- of-sel/what-is-the-casel-framework.

10 Zehr, H. 1990. *Changing lenses: A new focus for crime and justice.* Scottdale, PA: Herald Press.

courses refer them to SPED, or revert to outdated traditional methods of teaching. This also ties into our implicit bias,[12] from criminalizing hoodies to believing BIPOC[13] students need to be saved from their circumstances or surroundings. But I am not going to spend time getting into that in this book- feel encouraged to contact me for training to unpack further.

The Little Book of Restorative Justice in Education
also goes on to say that the tenets of restorative justice are based on two key beliefs:

1. Human beings are *worthy*.
2. Human beings are *interconnected* with each other and the world.

So, empathy plays a pivotal role in these values because the connection to others is what allows each one of us to feel emotions. Yet sadly, the challenge in building connection and showing worth occurs when someone does not believe that certain humans are worthy and deserving of those emotions. Yet sadly, the challenge in building connection and showing worth occurs when someone does not believe that certain humans are worthy and deserving of those emotions.

---

11. Evans, K. and Vaandering, D. 2016. *The Little Book of Restorative Justice in Education: Fostering Responsibility, Healing, and Hope in Schools*, 28. New York, NY: Good Books

12 Implicit bias is a form of bias that occurs automatically and unintentionally that nevertheless affects behaviors, judgments, and decisions.

13 BIPOC: Black, Indigenous, People of Color

This happens not just in our classrooms and schools, but in society as a whole. Countless examples of this exist, from the murder of George Floyd to the kicking out of Black students from a classroom for simple things like wearing a hoodie.

Regardless of someone's visual characteristics or their prior history, behaviors, or actions, each person is "of worth" simply because he or she is a living, breathing human being. Each human deserves to be given respect, dignity, and mutual concern.[14] -core values that surround the preceding beliefs of restorative thinking and perspective.

Now we know that no one is perfect, but perfection is never the goal. Some of us are hardwired to be more empathetic; many of us are not. Which means, just like anything else, empathy must be learned and practiced- not just one instance, but constantly. Recognizing social cues and understanding body language or tone of voice, or how one's own actions affect others, are the social-emotional skills worth spending time developing. And once we are able to become mindful and aware when we may not be giving respect or treating some- one worthy, it will be those moments when we must stop and check ourselves. Possibly ask: what message am I sending with my words, actions, body language? Such a question promotes empathy as well as compassion for others who share this Earth space same as you.

. . . .

We sometimes believe that our way of life is the only way to be lived; that our perspective is the "right" one. And although we should be living in our truth and feel confident in sharing it, remember that there are other truths that exist as well- so one must remain open. Especially for those who do not share the same cultures, values, or ways of life. Fostering empathy will help dismiss harmful and hurtful stereotypes. Once we do this, then we are able to remain and maintain a restorative way of life which nurtures healthy relationships, creates equitable environments, and resolves conflict without violence.

Sidenote: Students will follow your lead as you begin to set the tone for Circle. Showing your own vulnerability is essential. When you share personal, but not confidential, information about yourself, you are building trust within relationships. You cannot realistically ask something of your students that you are unwilling to do yourself. Being open and honest is super important. All of which will add to the creation of your emotional safe space learning environment.

---

14 Respect: "to look again" from the point of view of the other; Dignity: worth that cannot be substituted; Mutual Concern: reciprocal, interconnected concern

. . . .

Reconnection January

—

January 1st, in many countries across the world, signifies the New Year- and a new year means new goals and new aspirations. Although I tend to think of my Born Day as my own personal New Year, I love to make vision boards for the start of the calendar!

What exactly is a Vision Board, you may ask? Well, vision boards, to me, are a way to create and manifest your desires and wishes for the upcoming year as well as to hold one accountable for certain goals. You get a board or paper, tons of magazines or purchased scrapbooking books, scissors, glue, along with your positive attitude and get to work.

Personally, since like 7 years ago, I have created a vision board. I was partly influenced by my "sister", who started talking about it after watching the movie, *The Secret*. She was so excited about it that she even bought me a DVD copy of it, but I am ashamed to say that it is still in its original wrapper. Unopened. Unwatched. One day. One day...

But despite all of that, I have taken the concept of the vision board with me. Each year now my best friend, prays over my board because everything she places on hers seems to always come true, and I make sure to also have my manifestation candle, made by another dear friend, burning as well... as you can see, I play no games. And because I am such a visual person and believe in the power of spoken word and thoughts becoming action, I introduced vision boards within my classroom for my students (Lesson plan available on the website www.restorativerecipes.com)

Let me first say, you need A LOT of magazines to accommodate doing this activity with your students. But usually, at the end of the year, businesses are purging all of their old magazines so think about the ones you frequent and ask if they'd be willing to donate. Also, you can let people know on social media sites about your need; typically, there are a lot of individuals willing to donate any items to education. For primary grades, you may want your students to draw pictures, instead of cutting out images and words.

But Kyonna, I teach secondary so how can I do this with 130 students? The answer is easy lol... but it can be done as long as you dedicate the time. Typically, I started this activity on the first few days returning from Winter Break, because usually students return back on a Wednesday or Thursday. Or if you have Advisory, this is the perfect activity to do. That's what I did- but it was a collaborative effort because each Advisory in my grade level also participated. And what you definitely want to avoid is doing something totally cool and awesome with just one or two classes, and not all of them. So, I created an entire lesson plan accompanied with a rubric and all my students and I made vision boards. But the best part: presenting our vision boards in Circle.

Circle allowed us to not only share our goals, wishes, and ambitions, but we were able to reconnect with one another and tap back into the familial climate and culture we were accustomed to.

Shared Experience Moment

How do you spend time reconnecting with your students? How do they reconnect with one another? How do you reconnect with yourself?

- Are there any traditions or rituals? Phrases or Chants?
- I know time can be a challenge, but where can you make the time and space for reconnection moments and/or activities?

Restorative Recipe #7
Always Make the Time to Nurture Relationships

—

When a campus takes the time to intentionally dedicate time, opportunity, and energy to ensuring meaningful relationships are present, it truly affects the school's culture and its learning capabilities. A visitor can walk on campus and grasp an understanding of the culture, whether it is positive or not so positive.

One of the core concepts of a restorative community is addressing the needs of each person within the community. Even if unable to meet the need fully, simply acknowledging the need exists can offer comfort, which aligns with one's sense of safety. Carl Rogers and Abraham Maslow led the way in developing theories about human needs. These needs take precedence over any other thing and motivate behavior. And although it is sometimes mentioned in educational discussions and trainings, Maslow's 'Hierarchy of Needs' is not nearly talked about nor applied enough when it comes to understanding and supporting human behavior, for the youth and adults alike.

If a human does not have the basic needs of water, food, sleep, excretion, the primal instincts of survival are exemplified. Have you ever had to sit through a PD without having eaten lunch or even a snack to munch on? How did you feel while trying to learn? It was probably difficult to concentrate or listen to the speaker over the grumbles and rumbles of your tummy. Now just imagine if that were your reality daily. How much would you care about learning a new concept if you were hungry or sleepy? But this is our reality for many of our kids, and this reality is a constant, which does not allow focus on anything else.

Now once the basic, physiological needs are met, Maslow states that the next level of needs aligns with one's sense of safety. For our students, this level usually pertains to factors outside of their control as well as our own. Knowing that a home or job or resources of the family are secure falls within the realm within adult responsibility, in theory. But there are so many students that do not have stability and security of these things, and sometimes have to get these things on their own. Now we should already know that what happens outside of the four walls of our school building has a direct correlation to what happens within the four walls, despite us not having control of the external factors. However, when we keep this notion in mind, know that you do have control over making students feel safe and secure within the school walls. And it is paramount that ALL students feel this way. Many behaviors that impact bullying and ditching/skipping class revolve around a student's feeling of safety and security. And if we want our kids to be 'Upstanders' in our society, then we must model, pro- mote, and project such behavior.

The next two levels of the pyramid pertain to social needs and realizations. The third and fourth level are: Love/Belonging and Esteem. It is human nature for each one of us to desire love and belonging to a group. Now think about our students, particularly in secondary school. Some of them come to school not to learn academically, but to interact socially. And we know that romantic relationships can and will consume the lives of many of your students far more than we would like. Which is more reason to make time for social-emotional learning, relationship-building, and conflict resolution because it is far too much assumed that our students are able to reach these levels on their own, equipped with the appropriate skills, and be successful. Our responsibility is to teach and develop students' emotional intelligence because such behaviors are not inherent but learned.

A restorative environment seeks to make sure that everyone is treated with respect, dignity, and mutual concern regardless of any identity factors such as gender, race, ethnicity, sexual orientation, or ability. According to Maslow's pyramid, as well as other individuals who study human behavior, this is a natural human need of assurance. So, when any one human is deprived of these feelings, humans may respond in behaviors that will rebel against the "norm". Have you ever thought about why young people join gangs? For some, it's for protection (safety level), sometimes peer pressure or it's generational, and for others it is to simply belong to a group- to meet the need and fill the void of love and belonging to something outside of oneself.

Now I will admit that this generation is set up different when social interactions are involved. Social media has created disconnected and aloof youth; so social cues are missed, and emotions are disregarded, because nowadays you are able to hide behind a screen anonymously. Which is more the reason why educators should place just as much emphasis on people's dependence on one another, not their independence, as teaching any core content. Building healthy relationships should actually be the primary purpose of education. I know, I know... seems insane. But as I said before... how many intelligent yet out-of- touch folks do you see or hear about? *Emotional Intelligence is key*.

What constitutes a healthy relationship you may ask? One definition that I like describes a healthy relationship as when you "communicate respectfully and share power in a way that allows for individual and collective needs to be met.[15] Now, remember, that the word 'respect' means different things to different individuals. For that reason, I always encourage folks to know what certain words *look like* and *sound like* for each person.

Take cursing as an example. For some, cursing does not bother them. The delivery of the message does not get lost if you use an expletive. For others, even using a filler word, 'Dang', can be viewed as a disrespectful term. Some of our young people are allowed to curse at home, and it is not up to us to call their par- ents out. Instead, it is up to us to teach our students, and other young people around us, what is 'Situationally Appropriate'.[16] What is ok at home, or at church, or at the movies, or at your grandma's house, may not be appropriate at school- but we must teach this.

Another personal example stems from a regional cultural difference. I now live in the South, and it is a part of the culture to say 'ma'am' and 'sir'. Well, I am from Cali, and ummm, I definitely would prefer if you never "ma'am" me... *like ever*- adults and kids alike. Not that I don't appreciate or recognize the respect given using such terms, but I did not grow up like that. Therefore, it can take on a different meaning because such terms are used in different ways in different regions. So, this is why I push back on the 'Golden Rule' of: 'Treat others how you want to be Treated'. Instead, I say: 'Find out how others want to be treated and treat them that way.'

Once every person begins to consider how words and the delivery of messages directly impact how someone may view their own self-worth and dignity, then can the top level of Maslow's pyramid, which is Self-actualization, be achieved.

---

15 Zehr, H. The Little Book of Restorative Justice, pg. 62

16   Situationally Appropriate: behaviors that are viewed as acceptable in particular settings

Another popular pyramid that I would like to bring attention to is one that you are probably familiar with: the Multitiered Systems of Support (MTSS) or Response to Intervention (RTI) pyramid. This is a framework schools use to address academics and/or behavior through data-based decision-making. The pyramid emphasizes PBIS (positive behavior intervention & support) universal support and prevention-which is the base- as well as more individualized support for the other two tiers. Typically, the goal is to align academic standards with behavior expectations in order to enhance student performance. To give a little more detail:

- Tier I is School-wide and Universal. Preventative and Proactive. 100-80%
  o All settings. All students.
  o Restorative: Community-building. Social and Emotional Skill Development. Proactive Circles. Restorative language. Clear & Consistent High Expectations. Empathy-focused.

(Reaffirming Relationships)

- Tier II focuses on groups or within the classroom. 10-15%
  o Selective. More targeted.
  o Restorative: Small groups. Responsive Circles. Early Interventions. Communication Skills. Growth mind- set thinking.

(Repairing Relationships)

Humans 1st Students 2nd

....

- Tier III is individualized. 1-5%
  - o Modifications & Accommodations
  - o Restorative: Intensive & Specific. Re-entry Circle.

COSAs.

(Rebuilding Relationships)

Using the MTSS-model in isolation will not create the type of culture and climate you are looking for because if you wish to be truly restorative, understand that policies do not create the culture, but relationships do. And remember that relationships are the base and foundation of all things restorative. And I always say the wider the base, the narrower the tip. Relationships focus on individuals instead of lumping all students together-as is a common pitfall with a tiered-system. Schools are most restorative when students are engaged at ALL the levels of the pyramid. And if Circle is used on a regular basis as a communication tool, then everyone will become more familiar with the process and will be more likely to participate in more formal Circles if necessary. Just as importantly, restorative methods give a full picture of a student-not just academics. Incorporating restorative methods into the MTSS-model will make the appropriate space for social-emotional learning to take place as well as address unique student needs. Combined, this will truly enhance the school community along with student achievement.

Too many schools, however, operate in an "upside-

....

94

down" triangle, focusing on the tip more than spending intentional time establishing a solid foundation. One pushback about implementing Restorative is that it is time-consuming. And it is. Faculty and staff should be properly trained throughout the year. Modifications in the schedule need to be allotted for restorative practices on all tiers. Data collection needs to be consistent and constant. Behavior systems will need revision as data drives decisions and action planning. Sidenote: Data should not just be academically focused or about decreased referrals. It should reflect how students feel about the climate, policies, and daily routines, and most importantly, the existing relationships. The common saying is that "numbers don't lie", but we also have to consider the stories behind those numbers when deciphering meaning and before deciding the next steps.

Not putting the time in the beginning will have you for sure dealing with inappropriate behaviors more frequently throughout the entire year. And student success is our job and purpose, so the more time we dedicate to engaging in restorative practices, the easier the job will be as you will be able to create real change. Trust me- the investment of time is worth it.

Love Is... February

As previously stated, 'Love' (belonging) is an innate
desire of all humans. And it starts at a very young
age. From Pre-K babies wanting to stand close to
someone in the line or sharing a toy to high schoolers
possibly having babies of their own, love
is of major importance.

We tend to think of love only in a romantic sense;
however, love can be shared in many different types of
relationships, and I truly believe that is an important point
to make- especially for our middle schoolers.

When I did my one-year bid (lol) supporting a
middle school (shout out to all the 6th -8th grade
educators), I learned so much about how critical social-
emotional learning and emotional intelligence is for our
tweens at this point in their lives. I mean emotions run so
high and so intensely on all levels.

There was this one group of 7th grade girls that I will
never forget, for a variety of reasons. But mainly because
they taught me so much in terms of elevating my
emotional intelligence because I had to make sure that I
could properly help guide them through their constant
emotional roller coasters. And through this navigation, I
had to always remember that the social dilemmas that
plague our youth may not seem significant to me, as an
adult, but all were colossal events in their lives. So, I had

to learn not to minimize or dismiss while listening to students' stories because no student wants to be made to feel judged or that their problems are trivial compared to adulthood.

I remember one instance where I had to call a special circle together regarding 'Gossip'. To set the stage, I had just recently resolved a conflict between 4 of the 7-girl crew the week prior regarding food. Yes, you read that correctly.

As adults we may talk about the 5 Love languages, but our youth also have their own set of love languages as well. (I actually think there is a book about it). So, food for sure is a love language right. Well, one day one girl out of the crew bought chips for 3 girls in the crew but left out the 4th. And when I tell you that these girls were ready to FIGHT about what the one left out saw as disrespect and a diss! Thankfully, one of the other girls came to me so that I could intervene, and I sat them all down to safely share their feelings and soon they found out it was all a huge misunderstanding. The girl who had bought the chips only had a certain amount of money and also owed chips to 2 of the girls. The circle was a success as the 4 girls left my room laughing and hugging.

I was thrilled! And I thought that after that moment, there would not be any further issues. Well, I was wrong. Because I forgot the power of peer pressure and how so many students, particularly at this age, enjoy instigating and stirring the pot.

....

In about a week's time, while the 4 girls were still feeling connected, the other 3 girls, along with a string of random folks, began to start rumors about how each one of the 4 were really talking about one another behind each other's back. What started as just chatter in one class quickly spread to what seemed the entire school by midday. Which also meant a fight was probably on the horizon, because in their non-developed prefrontal cortex minds, any conflict must be resolved with violence.

Sidenote: I do not want to dive too deep into brain development, but it is definitely worth noting that brain development and what is seen as age-appropriate behavior must ALWAYS be considered when talking about behavior. According to research, the brain does not become fully developed until our 20s. And the pre-frontal cortex is the last portion to be completed. This is significant because the pre-frontal cortex is the part of our brains which serves as the center for impulse control and the ability to anticipate consequences. Since this is true, it also means that our youth are dependent on the other parts of their brain for decision-making, and those parts are associated with emotion and impulses. And since our youth have to be taught social-emotional skills, especially regulation and awareness, students will usually react, not respond, in a way that does not allow logic to play a part. Reactions are a direct result of the instant emotions created by the situation.

....

So, when I say, "Focus on the Behavior. Still love the Human", (a later chapter title) it is because our youth react mostly out of emotions of a moment more often than not, which is not a true reflection of who they are as a person or what they truly value. Keeping this in mind, and then taking the time to teach them different, which will increase their ability to respond versus react, will enhance their ability to become the empathetic, self-aware, and emotionally regulated individuals we want them to be.

Ok...back to the story.

I was walking the hallways when I overheard a young lady yell, "That chick said what? Oh, it's on!" I immediately recognized the voice and stopped her and the person she was talking to as they walked towards the locker room. "I need both of you to come with me now, please."

When we entered the room, I had each of them tell me what was happening, using Restorative Questions, I go into more detail about this next chapter and was able to gather enough information to know the gist of what was going on.

Sidenote: I always take notes when the students share, some people have students write down their "statements", but I have noticed that the older students get, the more reluctant they are to write information down- it's too much like snitching and fear it could be used against them in some way in the future. Of course, this could make students less likely to want to participate in the restorative process which as you very well know by now, is built on trust and mutual respect and is also voluntary. Therefore, you may want to caution on written statements. On the other hand, the process of writing can help our youth name their feelings and needs and lead them on a path of ownership of the situation. Bottomline: Use your own discretion as you know your students better than I do.

After hearing the two accounts, I realized that this could turn into a MAJOR problem quickly, so I quickly started to put together a plan of action for the group. It started with summoning the other 5 girls and 2 other girls who weren't apart of the group per se but were involved as their names came up a few times. And as always, I asked each of the girls if they were interested in participating in a Circle that would focus on the issue at hand. Out of the 9 girls, two said they were not completely comfortable, which I had to respect, but that also meant that I would have to develop an alternative agreement for those two that would complement the Circle process.

So, I prepared my Circle for 7 girls. Given the circumstances, I knew that I could possibly need some reinforcement, so I invited the counselor, who I worked closely with and a teacher that each of the girls had and who they said all had a great relationship with.

Sidenote: While preparing for your Circle, especially

one that is meant to resolve conflict or address a pressing issue amongst students, you may want to balance the youth to adult ratio. For one, this means you will not be the only adult responsible for supporting each of the girls with their needs and/or support plans. And for two, you never know if you'll need the backup if tension starts running high-which can happen. Sometimes, taking breaks or ending the Circle all together are the best options.

You may feel the need to take a break when participants are displaying a high range of emotion. I caution you with this if you're only doing this when things get uncomfortable because discomfort can represent growth and potential breakthroughs. We want to encourage and praise the communication! However, if a pause is necessary, especially for safety reasons, let participants know the process. If an individual needs to get up and take a break, choose a specific space and length of time. After the time expires, (no more than 2mins I think), you and/or the co- Circle Keeper needs to go check on the person and invite them to rejoin the Circle and continue the process. *If the person says no, the Circle must end!* Important to let the individual(s) know that the consequences will be different and possibly out of their or your control. More likely than not, the person returns.

I found the perfect talking piece, which was a picture of me and some of my crew from middle school (which they absolutely loved) and created the perfect Circle Script (also available on my website). I created the seating chart so that those who were beefing the most were not right next to one another, and that the one who seemed to be causing the most harm was sit- ting next to me on my left, which meant she was to go first. I was unable to do the Circle right away, which sometimes hap- pens, but arrangements were made to keep everyone separated and in non-communication until the next morning. And I must say that at the end of the Circle, again misunderstandings were clarified, and hurt feelings were comforted, and the girls made a pact amongst themselves to come to my class weekly to check-in with one another and to also come to me or the other two adults with any concerns so that things would not escalate like in this instance. And for the rest of the year, this girl group was able to navigate their emotions in a more constructive and mature manner. Of course, there were still issues, and times when more one-on-one chats were necessary, but fighting was off the table and disrespecting one another with curses or disparaging words definitely decreased. They would even approach me asking for a talking piece (which I tend to carry just in case) during break times or sign-up for the 'Restoration Space' to resolve issues on their own! Calling their own Circles!

And when the end of the school year came, I made sure to have a special Reflection Circle with the same group so that they could take the time to recognize their own personal growth as well as the growth in one another. And although I was not there the following year, I definitely like to think that they continued to build on those new social-emotional skills and possibly became role models to the lower grades. Because just as we do not think twice about how students begin reading on their own, we should also not be surprised when students use learned social skills on their own as well. Having them self- regulate and hold one another accountable is not just a utopian idea- it is very much a possibility.

Shared Experience Moment

In what moments can you enhance your students' emotional intelligence?

-   What topics or concerns can you address?
-   In what way can you bring your own personal experiences into the mix in order to share your thoughts or relate to the topic at hand?

Restorative Recipe #8
The Power of Circle

—

Whenever I conduct Circle, I know that the emotional safety of participants is just as important as physical safety. Up until this point, the restorative practices mentioned

have all been mostly informal in nature. Just like a lesson plan, any Circle needs a script and preparation, but remember there are different types of Circles. Therefore, for Circles that are considered Responsive, such as my 'Gossip' Circle or one on stealing (Tier and Re-entry Circles (Tier III-which I talk about in my April chapter), a trained facilitator should be the Circle Keeper. I also encourage that there are a few people on campus who have been trained just in case someone is absent or busy and a formal Circle is needed, because conducting Circle is a process.

Responsive Circles come after harm or conflict has occurred and are more formal than a Restorative conversation/chat. *Harm* is sometimes thought to be an intentional act that causes physical pain. But harm is much more than that. Harm can be emotional or mental, even spiritual. It is anything that makes a person feel less than or their worth questioned or minimized, regardless of intent. I always say that there is a difference between Intent vs. Impact. Regardless of how you meant to say or do something, the way it impacted someone is what truly matters.

Similarly, conflict does not equate with violence. Which is a common thought. And conflict is inevitable within relationships where there is mutual concern for one another. In fact, it is a complex relational interaction because without mutual concern for one another, any negative interaction between individuals may begin to present itself as personal attacks. Conflict and harm are violations of people and relationships, not rules and laws. With this in mind, and I have said this already, *you cannot restore a relationship that does not already exist*, so make sure your foundation is set and your community is built. As Pranis notes, formal restorative practices define justice as *getting well* not *getting even*.[17]

Preparation

Once harm occurs or conflict arises, the person(s) responsible must prepare for Circle. The steps to prepare for a Responsive Circle should mirror the following process:

- Gather the initial facts: sequence of events, who was
- involved, past incidents, relationship dynamics, etc.

Once you know all the involved parties, gather information from each potential participant. I use the word 'potential' because remember participation in the restorative process is voluntary. As you listen to each side of the stories, make sure to write down their accounts and ask the same guiding Restorative Questions so that you remain as objective as possible. The authors of *Hacking School Discipline* provide a helpful tool for learning a student's perspective is recapping the student's personal account of what happened, and then move on to a prompting question, such as, "So you only looked at him once, and he threw a pencil at you?" This allows the student to slow down and realize there may be more to the story.[18] They suggest also encouraging students to share everything, because if not then the situation can- not be fully resolved and could possibly have different consequences later on.

- o   To add, when speaking with those who have been harmed, I add a few more questions that express my care and concern for their well-being. Such questions might be:

  - Are you alright?

  - Is there anything you need right now at this moment?

  - How can I help?

  - What did you think when you realized what had happened?

  - What has been the hardest thing for you?

---

17 Pranis, K. 2003. Peacemaking Circles: from crime to community. St. Paul, MN. Living Justice Press

o   Sidenote: I always ask those I speak with if there is anyone that they would like as a 'support person' and anyone that would make them feel uncomfortable. You, as the Circle Keeper, should never be any- one's support person. Generally, adults should be seen as impartial, but in some cases, a student may have a strong connection with a coach, teacher, or custodian, so including them in the Circle, can allow for a safer space.

Once you get to this point, you ask the question: Are you willing to participate in a Circle to address what has happened? If either the 'responsible youth or those harmed say 'No', the Process STOPS HERE! You must find an alternative form of resolving the conflict.

- After hearing each person's story and learning of possible motivations for behavior and the effect on others it has had, you can decide how formal the Circle should be. Sometimes after talking to folks, you may decide that a smaller conference fits best because it seemed to be a simple misunderstanding based on assumptions, misin- terpretations, or past interactions. In other instances, you may decide that parents or other stakeholders[19] need to be part of the process, which of course, takes more planning for time and space.

---

18 Maynard N. and Weinstein B. 24. Hacking School Discipline. (Ways to create a Culture of Empathy & Responsibility Using Restorative Justice. 2020. Highland Heights, OH. Times Ten Publication.

....

- ○ Choose an appropriate location and make sure to have enough time to allow the process to go through all the necessary steps and for participants to fully be heard without limitations. These types of Circles take time and patience and cannot be rushed or forced.

- ○ This next step is essential to a Circle's success and that is preparing each participant for what Circle will look and sound like. You want to discuss the guidelines and other expectations such as sharing and actively listening. You want each person to know that this is not a discussion nor debate nor attack-this is about taking ownership over our choices and healing so we can move forward.

  - ○ Sidenote: For those who have been harmed, I always ask what if the responsible youth does not take full responsibility for the harm or cannot give you what you need, what then? And I found this to be really instrumental and a social learning moment because I never force apologies or give students "the answer"- this is a fluid, authentic process.

---

19 A stakeholder is anyone who participated in or has been affected by the choices and behaviors

....

- Create a seating chart: I personally go to the left with my Circles, because that is what side our heart is on, and it is how the blood flows through the body which to me keeps us interconnected on a deeper human level. With this in mind, I am extremely intentional about who sits where when facilitating a Responsive Circle. The person to my left will always speak first, so as previously mentioned, I tend to place the person who was responsible for the harm to the left of me. From experience I have learned that if the responsible youth speaks last, listening to other's perspective may feel like he or she or they are being ganged-up on, which can cause them to shut down and not want to participate. Having them speak first also reiterates that the restorative process is not about shaming or punishing, but for healing and understanding.

- I will usually place their selected support person or another affected person next to the one who caused harm. Then place an adult to break up the student voices and to continue this until the one who was most harmed is placed to the right of me, also keeping in mind personalities and potential stresses and/or anxiety. *You never want to place these two people in direct eye contact with one another because it can cause more harm than good and possibly escalate the situation. Also, if support people are causing more issues, you can always tell them to leave.*
  - Sidenote: For proactive circles, you may

decide to do a seating chart so that students who always sit near each other and may be a distraction are separated. Or you may put the student who likes to speak a loooootttttttt, is one of the last ones to share so that everyone has an opportunity to share because time is always a factor.

- Select a meaningful talking piece: try to choose a talking piece that is related to the topic or holds some type of significance or connection to the group. You never want to pick a random object to be your talking piece, such as a marker or pen, as this can take away its importance. A Talking Piece also is an equalizer as it neutralizes any power imbalances that may exist, which is another reason why it should be special in some way. You may want to have participants bring their own Talking Piece and have a Circle about that topic. Then, those who feel comfortable, can keep their Talking Piece in the middle to become part of the Centerpiece or used as a future

Talking Piece. And just as any one person wants their object respected, it emphasizes the need to respect others' possessions.

- Arrange the room: make sure that chairs/seats are placed in a Circle without any type of desks or other fixtures (if possible). The shape of the Circle is symbolic as it illustrates transparency and equality- there is no front of the line or sharp corners. It is continuous with no end, which links everyone together even at different positions within the Circle. It suggests that everyone sitting within chooses to participate and shares ownership of the process because I would always say that the Circle can only be as great as those who choose to verbally contribute. The shape has metaphorical meaning as well. As Indigenous people point out, the earth is a circle. Our head is a circle, there are circle shapes all over the human body as well as in plants and animals.[20]

Although it is not essential to holding Circle, having a Centerpiece definitely helps establish the sacredness of Circle and also can provide a physical representation of the Circle community. Place the Centerpiece in the center of the Circle. The Centerpiece should contain significant objects relating to yourself and the community/class/group. Here is a place for your values and other Circle-created documents/activities to be placed. I personally like to include some type of flower or plant to connect us to the natural world and of course a box of tissues. I will usually let participants know that the Centerpiece serves as a place for eyes to go if making eye contact makes them uncomfortable and also a place for our shared stories and voices to be collected.

20 Riestenberg, N. 2012. *Circle in the Square Building Community and Repairing Harm in School*, 75. St. Paul, MN: Living Justice Press

Process

You or another trained adult may serve as the Circle Keeper. As the Circle Keeper you are there to guide the conversation, not control it, and encourage participants to share their truth. In the beginning or for those new to Circle, I would always ask the question and then share my response to set the tone. But I would sometimes share last as to not influence anyone's answer- remember what people say is their truth- there is no right or wrong answers. Your primary goal as the Circle Keeper is to make everyone feel safe and facilitate the flow of the dialogue.

The general format of Circle remains the same for the most part; it's the content that changes depending on the type of Circle. The format is as follows:

1. Welcome/Purpose: You may want to have music playing or use a common ritual like a sound bowl or bell to signify the start of the Circle.

Thank everyone for coming and for their participation in advance. Give purpose of the Circle.

-   In this particular instance, provide an overview of the situation and state that the goal is to repair the harm by making things as right as possible through steps previously discussed. Encourage verbal participation but uphold the Guidelines. This should not be a Circle of Blame, but a Circle of Resolution

Review Guidelines and Talking Piece and Centerpiece (optional):

2. Guidelines should focus on and be similar to the following:
   i. Respect the Talking Piece (One mic)
   ii. Let your Heart Guide you
   iii. Listen Actively with your Heart
   iv. Participate with Respect
3. Here is a great place to talk briefly about body language. I always mention that verbal communication is only 7% which means the other 93% is everything else: tone, facial expressions, body language. All of which can speak much louder than words. The wrong body language can turn any type of well-intended conversation into an unproductive and possibly hostile situation

a. Sidenote: have a Circle about this topic which will enhance self-awareness

i. What is Said Here, Stays Here so Keep our Stories Safe[21]

---

21 This guideline is critical to build trust, but many of us are man- dated reporters which means we must let participants know that if any- thing is shared that says someone is harming them, harm- ing some- one else, or thoughts of harming self, then an outside conversation must be had.

....

a. Keeping confidentiality promotes honest con-
    versation while developing empathy, connection,
    respect, trust, and caring. Important to discuss how
    you can share the story of Circle, but not personal
    details, unless permission was given to do so

b. To ensure that all involved have the same expectation
    of confidentiality, Circle Keepers can ask, "What will
    we tell others about this Circle?"[22] No one wants to
    feel like what they have shared in Circle will then be
    used against them socially later

    i.   Talking Piece should always be something
         significant to the people participating in the
         Circle or relevant to the topic. NEVER something
         random like a pen or marker

    ii. Centerpiece (if permissible)

2. Check-In: Use one of the Check-in questions to gage
   where your participants are before starting Circle.
   This way you have an idea of the level of readiness
   from each person

3. Opening: I like to use a poem, quote, or some other
   related content that directly connects with the reason
   the Circle is happening

a. Keep in mind the diversity that exists within your
    par- participants when choosing content so that all feel
    included and/or seen/represented

---

22 Riestenberg, N. 2012. *Circle in the Square Building Community and Repairing
Harm in School*, 108. St. Paul, MN: Living Justice Press

....

4. Storytelling Round: You always want an opportunity to have everyone share a story about themselves that is related to the larger conversation. This allows for everyone to connect and relate with one another before addressing the situation in a natural way while also creating a pathway for developing empathy.

5. Discussion rounds: Depending on the type of Circle, these questions will be varied. But since this chapter is about harm and conflict, the following example will focus on that type of Circle.

   Start with the person responsible for the harm begin first with sharing their perspective. I like to go to the left, because that is what side our heart is on and how the blood flows through our body, so the 'responsible youth' should be sitting to your left. Then you go around the Circle to others who had been directly harmed by the incident to share their perspectives.

a. You want to have the Restorative Questions guide you so that you already have an idea of what each person is going to say due to the previous interviews

b. Before asking about how to make things as right as possible, I like to ask these questions:

   i. What role did you play or how did you contribute to this conflict?

   ii. What does each person need from those in the Circle to be able to resolve this conflict as much as we can?

1. You may come to find that multiple people have reasons to acknowledge their role in the conflict and make things right

    iii. What needs to be done now to make things as right as possible?

1. As each person shares, take note as this will become the agreement and obligations. As Howard Zehr notes, "Violations create obligations. The central obligation is to put right the wrong."[23] You may want to have everyone come to a consensus regarding these obligations, or at minimum a compromise.

6. Check-out Round: this can take several forms. You may want to use the same question you asked in the Check-in Round. Or you may want participants to share a word or phrase, Connection, or

7. Closing: Just as you open the Circle, you should close the Circle as well. I usually like to use a Unity Clap or have each person turn to their neighbors and say, "Thank you for your participation."

Follow-Up

This step is sadly sometimes disregarded or treated with the least focus- but it is the accountability piece, so it is essential. At the end of Circle, an agreement should be constructed where participants state agreed upon actions, support people, and timelines. Checking in with participants the next day and days to follow is also helpful. You want to make sure that everyone is also meeting their obligations agreed upon in the Circle so that needs are met and resolution is achieved. Surveys indicate that Circle agreements and Restorative Conferencing agreements are completed 95-100 percent of the time.[24] Much of the success can be contributed to the clear expectations expressed in the Circle process, the involvement of everyone affected, and everyone's voice reflected in the agreement. Make sure to also set up a follow-up meeting around 2-3 weeks after the initial Circle to celebrate progress and discuss any necessary revisions to make certain that the old conflict no longer is an issue and address any potential problems, before they become major.

Using restorative measures, instead of traditional methods, allows students to reconnect with those around them and to establish reconnection with their school community.

And when given the opportunity to show up, display responsibility, and be true to their word, the majority of youth will do so-we just have to give them a chance to.

23 Zehr, H. *The Little Book of Restorative Justice*. 19

24 Ierley, A. and Ivker, C."Restoring School Communities: A Report on the Colorado Restorative Justice in Schools Program," Research and Practice Insert, *Voma Connections* 13 (Winter 2003); Legal Rights Center Grantee Report, 2011

Humans 1st Students 2nd

....

March Madness March

Generally, the title of this chapter makes the majority of folks think of basketball; but when it comes to schooling, this generally means that just about everyone on campus is about ready to foul out the game. Tempers are high. Patience is thin. Stress is Real.

I will never forget this one particular day when we were having an event in the quad at lunch. Clubs and the SEL team had set up booths to promote the theme for the month so there was this electric charge in the air that everyone could feel. Just about the entire school, which had 438 students at the time, were located in the same area- which also included about 6 girls who should not have been near one another.

Allow me to provide some background context: there were a group of young ladies, majority were 9th graders, that sadly were having difficulty getting along with one another. There were: sub-disses[25] happening on all social media platforms, glares and mad-dogging[26] happening in the halls and common areas, and constant mumbles and talking mess during class.

---

25 Sub-diss: when you make implications about someone without explicitly stating who they are
26 Mad dogging: staring as though you were crazy; threatening glance

Now, being that this event was in March, I had a solid rapport with each one of those 6 girls and was also a part of the team who put supports and resources in place for a few of them who needed it. I had the numbers of their parents, guardians, or other important adults in my phone, and each of them had participated in Circles before, whether with me personally or within their classrooms. Each knew the school's expectations as well as my own personal ones when it came to their choices and behavior, because we focused on them weekly. There had even been some smaller prior interactions that required intervention and agreements. But something about this day... brought the madness out.

I was at one of the tables, with a few of my students from my *Kings & Queens* club, including 2 girls out of the 6 men- mentioned above. We were talking about their day and how each of them had been handling the conflicts, when out of the corner of my eye, I saw 3 of my other girls walking our way, towards the table. I smiled at them and waved- because the last thing you want any of your students to think is that you are taking sides or playing favorites, because the moment that happens, trust and connection is lost. As my arm descended back to my side, I whisper to the 2 in front of me, "Keep looking and talking to me .G and Z are walking this way but remember what we talked about." But in the pit of my stomach, I had an ominous feeling. In retrospect, I wish I would have immediately walked with those 2 girls to another part of campus, or had them sit behind the table with me, because what happened next is something I never expected...

As all 3 girls walked by the table, 1 of them decided to turn around and walk straight to me. She "politely" pushed her way through the crowd and came around the back of the table to give me a hug.

"Heeeeyyy, Ms. Hardy," she shouted as she gave me a hug, "Your favorite student is here."

"Hi G. How are you today? Everything all good?" I asked as I looked her in the eyes with that "Momma look" and eye- brows up.

"Of course, Ms. Hardy. I am having a fabulous day, espe- cially with my ridahs who always got my back."

"Awesome. Well keep enjoying your fabulous day with your ridahs. Tell them I said 'hello' and that I'll be checking in on ya'll a little later. And as always, I want you to continue making the best choices you can."

"I got you Ms. Hardy," she said as she stepped backward a few steps and then turned to walk away, smiling.

Now, in hindsight, I believe that was sent over as a pos- sible distraction so that I wouldn't interfere with the previously planned plan of events of her and her "ridahs", because no sooner than I looked down at the table, I hear a wave of stu- dent voices and see a rush of students running in one direction. Immediately, I knew a fight was happening.

I rushed from behind the table and maneuvered my way to the center of the now multiple dozens of gathered students, to see not 1 or 2, but 5 of MY GIRLS fighting!

And without hesitation, I jumped right in there too.

As I was trying to separate the girls, I was yelling their names, hoping they realized I was now in the mix and would stop punching each other. I would say it kinda worked as after about 30 seconds the fight was over. But if you have ever been in a fight or witnessed one, you know that 30 seconds is a looonnnggg time for a fight. As I got up from the ground, (yes I said the ground), I didn't see any of my girls, but I did see all the adults you would imagine who would show up when a brawl breaks out. As I began to realize what had fully occurred, I looked down to see that I was missing my shoe. And my keys. A hoop earring. And my phone.

"Here's your keys Ms. Hardy." A student handed me my lanyard. "Thank you. Keep a look out for my black Chuck please. Oh, and my phone. And a gold hoop, but I can always get more at the Slauson." The student laughed. "Iight, bet."

I limped back to the Student Center- a large room that had desks for all the support personnel for our students such as the Counselors and Social workers and me. But no sooner than I had sat down in my chair, I was asked to go to the school campus police office. Still shoeless, phoneless, and hoopless, I limped to the office, where I gave my account of what happened and was given an ice pack for my eye and chin, since I took a few elbows. Once I finished there, the Administration team was waiting for me, to seek input on how to move forward with consequences. I truly appreciated the ask, as even in the midst of one of the largest fights that school year, the Admin team was still dedicated to walking the Restorative path.

They had already sent all the girls involved home, which for safety reasons, was the best thing to do. And in a Traditional school setting, they would have gone home with mandatory suspensions. But again, my Admin team was dedicated to remaining Restorative, so they came to me for the next steps, which was such a pivotal move. So, I went over the process again for them that should take place after harm occurs; the first step was getting each girl's perspective of what happened, as well as some bystanders, and allies to each side if possible. The reason for this is because if a Harm Circle were to occur, you want to make sure that whoever would be a part of it was a part of the process from the beginning-but we'll talk more about that in the next section.

So, I spent the rest of the day calling my 6 girls, because hearing their side while it was fresh and without possible influences for false collaborations was a critical piece. And being that it was a Friday, the sense of urgency was intensified. The rest of the Admin team spent the rest of the day speaking to bystanders and of course since this is a generation of social media- they were able to discover the fight on camera.

Now, when I was collecting statements, I made sure to stick to the core 5 Restorative Questions, so that there was no bias or subjectivity. And what the 3 told me, I later would find out (mostly due to the video footage) was a complete BOLD FACE LIEEEEEEEE!

To get to the gist of it, I was told that the fight was 1-on-1. It wasn't until 1 of my 2 girls (from the table) jumped in, that the other girls jumped in too. Well, that was completely untrue. And when they returned to school on the Monday after, to participate in a Restorative ISS session, they all lied to MY FACE until I told them I saw the video.

Their faces went from victory to defeat, as they realized they had been caught, but I expressed to each of them how not only was I deeply disappointed in all of their choices, but that I honestly felt betrayed, hurt, and foolish for believing their versions of the story. And I told them that they might be feeling all righteous and justified in that moment, but the consequences of their actions would go far beyond that day. And, sadly, the relationship I had with each of them would be altered for an extremely long time. And in the days, even weeks, to follow, they felt it-as our relationship became very surface after that. And it became that way because the trust and respect I believed existed between each of us was violated.

Broken. And to get back to the place where we were would have taken more time than we had, as I moved to another state at the end of the school year.

I still think about each of them often though. Because I knew all they had overcome to get to the space we had been before the fight. So, if they ever read this, just know Ms. Hardy has always and will always be your Mama Bear who loves you and I hope that life after high school has been great for you thus far.

Shared Experience Moment

Think of a time when you felt betrayal or hurt from a student?

- What happened?
- How did that change the relationships/dynamics between you and them?
- Were you able to heal and move past it?
- How did you this experience prepare you for future disappointments?

Restorative Recipe #9
Focus on the Behavior. Still love the Human

—

I'm sure that after reading the anecdote for this chapter, a great many of you probably thought the phrase, some even said it out loud: 'They should have *known* better!' All too often we assume that our youth have the appropriate social skills to navigate conflict and once the body's natural defense mechanism of 'fight, flight, or freeze' activates, logic and sometimes practiced skills go out the window. At the end of the day, whether a person instinctively reacts or deliberately chooses an action, 'knowing better' comes with intentional practice. Remember, emotional regulation is not inherent; it is learned. And most times, our students have not been taught how to effectively communicate what they are feeling. But if the person believes that the reasons for their actions are justified all the practice in the world will not matter. Because you must realize that life is not binary-there is not simply one 'right' or 'wrong' choice; no 'good' or 'bad'.

Life is all shades of grey. And choices come in a range. Which is also why we must separate the behavior from the person.

In a traditional sense, our justice system is set up in a very linear way. There is the offender and the victim. A crime and a punishment. There are mandatory minimums and little, if any, room for explanation or understanding. Sadly, or school systems are similar in structure as we see this where the following three questions are usually asked:

1. What rule was broken?
2. Who broke it?
3. What is the punishment?

With this one-size-fits-all way of thinking, usually the victim is not even considered, included, or mentioned. The two parties are detached and separate. And there is no lasting change because behavior is forced. Essentially, the school-to- prison pipeline, which mainly affects marginalized groups, is reinforced. And we must realize how mishandling our reaction to inappropriate behaviors can greatly affect a student's life in a variety of ways outside of their educational journey.

In contrast, within a restorative community, the justice system is a full-circle experience. Everyone who was affected by the harm, as well as the person(s) who caused the harm, and the person(s) harmed are all equally included in the process of making things as right as possible. The process focuses on healing, not on further hurt and harm.

*Sidenote: notice how the language I used changed from criminalizing to validating. Restorative practices include restorative language; but the words we choose should always be deliberate and in support of the ultimate goal. Using language that promotes unity, dignity, and respect amongst every individual part of the community is key. Because at some point in our life, we can, and will, be in any of the above mentioned positions.

So instead of using the traditional three questions after a harm occurs, remember the restorative questions for the 'responsible youth' should be:

1. Can you tell me what happened, step-by-step?
2. What were you thinking about at the time? How did you feel?
3. Who has been affected by what you did? How are they affected?
4. How do you feel now about what happened?
5. What needs to happen now to make things as right as possible?
6. In the future, if something similar is happening, what can you do differently?

Carolyn Boyes-Watson and Kay Pranis, authors of *Circle Forward*, point out that 'justice' is not about laws [rules] or any defined behaviors, but instead about relationships. They point out that humans naturally have an innate sense of things that are just and equitable. When our relationships begin to feel unjust, we can sometimes build up "negative emotions, such as anger, resentment, distrust, and humiliation". On the flip side of that, when relationships are felt as just ["right"], we go through a "sense of harmony, peace, stability, and satisfaction."[27] Establishing an equitable environment consists of meeting the needs of the individuals in it. And ultimately, a truly just and fair environment.

Too often, we associate the word 'fair' with 'equal', which in fact is not accurate. Equality gives this false belief that if everyone is treated exactly the same, it would level out the playing field. However, we all know that every person does not start in the same position in life. That every experience is perceived differently, and the injustices of the world play a major part. Institutionalized oppression and harm are realities. And unfortunately, all of these factors are not considered in traditional school systems, which data has proven to show disparities and disproportionalities particularly among our Black and brown babies, SPED students, and most recently our LGBTQ+ youth as well. We cannot ignore the complexities and layers that exist outside of the four walls of our school, because what affects each of us in the outside world directly impacts our school life. We must strive for 'Equity'.

27 Boyes--Watson, C., and K. Pranis. 2015. *Circle Forward*, 139. St. Paul, MN: Living Justice Press

....

Consider the anecdote at the beginning of this chapter. Each one of the girls involved in that altercation had different rea- sons for fighting. And even though sitting them all down in a Circle would have probably been a set-up for another rumble, I did take the time to talk to each of them to better understand their reasons and to hear what she believed to be the best way to make things as right/just as possible. And after our conversations, we developed agreements to honor so that each one of them could exist without fear or drama. Some of them even chose to squash the beef, which came with later smaller circles and me providing and encouraging the skills necessary to set boundaries. Remember, restorative practices seek to make sure that when harm or conflict occurs, the needs of all those who have been impacted are met in ways that restore what has been broken.

Remember: everyone has their OWN perception of jus- tice. And perspective is reality. You never have to share the same ideas as anyone you have a dialogue with nor agree with actions. But you must make the effort to understand "what happened" to influence their choices- this is the only way to be able to move forward effectively. We have to stop trying to "fix" student behavior while ignoring the underlying contexts. Keep in mind that behavior comes from somewhere. Therefore, we should engage with our students so underlying needs can be addressed. The incident is the symptom, the context is the cause.

....

And I know now that many of you are waiting for me to tell you how each girl was punished. Because a common argument for those who push back on restorative approaches is that there is no consequence for misbehavior. Which is a major misconception!

Restorative approaches allow for consequences as part of the accountability process. However, what restorative does not do is *punish*. And 'consequence' and 'punishment' do not mean the same thing-they are not interchangeable. The criminal jus- tice system punishes. Parents punish. Restorative communities *teach*.

Commonly, I know that it is a general consensus that punishment plays an important role in shaping behavior, but honestly if punishment (traditional methods) worked, then there would not be any discipline concerns within our educational systems because punitive measures have been used since the creation of school. But we all know this is not the case.

Why is this? Because punitive measures do not teach!

In fact, punishment usually causes resentment and anger, causing one to feel disconnected from their environment. Not to mention that punishment as an intervention does not align with how we are biologically wired. Shame is a dominant affect that our young people are quite susceptible to, which accord- ing to psychiatrist Donald Nathanson shows up in four different ways: attacking others, attacking self, withdrawal, and avoidance.[28] Dr. James Garbino, a psychologist who

....

studies the causes of violence in children, traces violent behavior to feelings of shame and humiliation. Think about any instance where a student has acted out in a violent way. Were there other people around? Did you later find out the events leading up to behavior? Or in hindsight, were there cues to show the student was feeling angry or frustrated? According to Dr. Garbino, if a child feels humiliated, especially in front of peers or friends, all energy goes into dealing with those feelings by trying to cover them up and save face. Then, we have some students who do not struggle with shame at all and may act out in all of their entitled glory. And then we may also have students who have experienced trauma, which then adds another layer of complexity.

According to a report titled *Responding to Childhood Trauma: The Promise and Practice of Trauma Informed Care*, Gordon R. Hodas, MD states that students who have experienced trauma need "unconditional respect." Yes, you read that right! UNCONDITIONAL... Adults need to make sure and take extreme care that traumatized youth not be challenged "in ways that produce shame and humiliation." And since we have no idea what traumas our students have lived through or are living through, we must use universal precautionary practices grounded in humanistic approaches.

---

28 Riestenberg, N. 2012. *Circle in the Square Building Community and Repairing Harm in School*, 30. St. Paul, MN: Living Justice Press

....

Sadly, this is not happening in the majority of our schools. In a traditional setting, students are punished through exclusionary measures-which is actually counterproductive when attempting to change behavior. And in most instances, the only lesson learned from punishment is to do better next time with misdeeds so that he or she doesn't get caught. There is no thoughtful reflection and usually a lack of or denial of responsibility because no one wants to get in trouble. The opportunity to build empathy is taken away because there is no conversation, and the root cause of the issue goes unaddressed, which also means that needs are not met, thus only applying a "band-aid" to the wound. And really punishing our students can come across as adults trying to "leverage an unequal power relationship over children; it puts children in their places by reminding them who's *really* in charge."[29] Research shows that suspensions produce problematic outcomes and clearly contribute to the school-to-prison pipeline.[30] However, I do realize that at times suspension is needed, especially to allow for cool-down time and for adults to plan the next steps. But I am also say- ing that this should be used in limitation and not be the norm. Because when schools seek to punish through suspension,

29 Fisher. N and Fisher. D and Smith. D. 2015. *Better Than Carrots or Sticks Restorative Practices for Positive Classroom Management.*
30 Alexandria, VA: ASCD The Advancement Project. 2010. *Federal Policy, ESEA Reauthorization, and the School to Prison Pipeline.*

detention, expulsion, you are in fact working against any and all ideas that promote unity, connection, and togetherness the very values any community would want to teach and live by.

But in a restorative community, regardless of past indiscretions, people are embraced. The person who was harmed is not looked as a mere victim, passive in the process; but instead, looked to as someone who can help repair the harm, or offer insight about the incident, and who is essential to finding resolution. In addition, the person who caused harm is not shunned by the community, but instead is reminded that although their behavior is unacceptable, they are still cared about. And still belong to the community. Which is why despite the need to have healthy space, and for some the appreciated break, it is crucial to have those who cause harm returned back to their environments much sooner than later so that the process of repairing relationships can begin and academic learning can continue.

Living restoratively means continual commitment to upholding everyone with respect, dignity, concern, and support. Restoring the connections and relations in meaningful ways is key. Including the consequences-all of which will align with the harm so that true accountability and restoration is possible. If this does not occur, and because of our natural need to want to belong to a group, you will find yourself dealing with a group of individuals who have bonded over the feelings of push-out and marginalization.

Another quick story: when one of my 7yr-olds ran through the hallway, pulling down the work and ripping the decorations, not only did I have that baby go through the hallway and staple (with my help) and tape back the items he destroyed, but he also had to go into each of the classrooms and apologize to the students and teacher.

This, of course, was agreed upon after the student had calmed down (because you cannot have a productive conversation when someone's central nervous system is still hyper-activated. And repeating the phrase, "Use Your Words" will prove ineffective if the person does not have the skillset to do so.) and we were able to have a restorative conversation, which also included meeting the needs of the student who expressed all the antecedent events prior to his eruption. In the end, his consequence served not as punishment, but as a way to authentically reconnect with those around him. And might I add that the consequence is directly linked to the behavior, which is logical.

Logical consequences have more of an emotional investment which in turn will help change behavior. Had he been suspended, the opportunity to figure out what motivated his behavior in that moment would have been lost. And again, looking for the motivation (function) of a behavior and trying to understand it does not mean that you are excusing or rationalizing it. However, failing to look at the misbehavior on a deeper level will prevent us from identifying proper interventions and/or supports to truly meet the needs of the student and discover the underlying issue(s). Use the "iceberg metaphor" where you know the above-water peak is just a small portion of what really lies underneath the surface. Outbursts and attitudes are rarely attempts to manipulate a situation, but rather an indication that a skillset is missing or underdeveloped. And other factors such as gender norms and cultural expectations can play a major role in this as well.

For our youth to be able to experience the highest levels of success, they must be taught the skills needed to get there.

Thus, teaching, listening, and learning is vital. And remember that making mistakes is a normal and, really, a valuable part of growing up. Too often we attempt to control students' behavior rather than teach them how to make the best choices.

So much can be achieved when we know more about what comes before the behaviors, we find problematic, especially when that may be the first time that circumstance had occurred. Restorative practices are effective because they turn every conflict into a learning opportunity. Let's always strive to help turn missteps into steps towards healthy development.

"If we have a better understanding of how the brain works, how affect and emotion are generated in the CNS [central nervous system], what behaviors they motivate, the social and self-regulation skills that we want taught, and can overcome barriers to participation in our responses, then it makes sense to move toward restorative approaches as the most effective approach to problem-solving."[31]

31 Burnett, N., and M. Thorsborne. 2015. *Restorative Practice and Special Needs*, 60. Philadelphia, PA: Jessica Kingsley Publishers

April Showers... April

—

When I moved to the South, my position placed me in an elementary school. Now having the 8 years of experience. I had working with teenagers, I figured that children would be a breeze. And let me tell you... I was SO WRONG!

Never did I ever think that I would be cursed out by a 4-year-old nor punched on by a 6-year-old; bit, kicked, furniture launched at you name it -and it happened. It almost sent me packing back to Cali that first year-no lie. Nobody warned me that elementary school was set up like that! But after some major pep talks and forming strong bonds with like-minded folks who became my Squad (which is essential to have in teaching), I embraced the opportunity to continue to do the work with restorative practices at the forefront.

Notice I said forefront, because restorative practices are not the end all be all it works in collaboration with other factors such as PBIS, SEL, DEI, and trauma-informed care

I will never forget one of my 5th graders who came to us after the school year had started, which means that the opportunity to form meaningful relationships and connections with his peers and the adults on campus was cut shorter than the majority. And the reason for this is because he had transferred from another school-an opportunity transfer.

Now, I want you to take a second to write down the first words, phrases, or ideas that came immediately to mind when you read the words "opportunity transfer" ...

Because just like the file record that follows each student, that phrase has negative connotations and implications too. And that really sucks... because it places labels on our students before he or she or they even walk through the door.

I'll never forget his day of arrival because the whispers in the halls and offices were rampant, and the apprehension of his teachers' faces was evident. I knew too much about him already without ever meeting him. Sad how that happens. But I am a huge advocate of a 'clean slate'; a daily one at that because you never know if someone wakes up in the morning with a new attitude and commitment to life. So, with this in mind, I wanted to make sure that this student saw me as one of the adults in his life that was in his corner and support of his betterment.

I had created a tradition at that school site where with every new student, I had the opportunity to meet them while also introducing them to Community Circles (Tier 1 practice) by having each new person participate in our 'Welcome Circle' (Circle Script available on website). The 'Welcome Circle' was an opportunity to learn new facts and feelings about our new community members as well as for them to get to know some of the adults and Administrators on campus. I remember him being very quiet, cautious even, of those around him. He was reluctant to share, which was fine, but I knew that connecting with him might prove a challenge.

And needless to say, a challenge he was. Almost daily, if not hourly it seemed, I was being called to assist with him as he was being written up for all kinds of incidents. And soon I began to realize that the adults around him were gathering the necessary documentation to send him off to DAEP- Discipline Alternative Educational Placement.

Sidenote: the concept of DAEP was a very new concept to me and a place that I still equate to almost a baby juvenile hall. It is directly connected to the School-to-Prison Pipeline, and although I realize that some students can and do benefit from alternative environments, it's the purpose and intention behind the setting that determines whether it will be truly beneficial to helping our youth grow and learn from their choices.

Back to the story.

When students participate in certain actions, such as fighting, many school districts operate under a mandatory punishment requirement. (Sounds very familiar to mandatory sentencing right). And regardless of the 'why' behind the choice, the DAEP is the mandatory placement. Without going too deep into the personal history and underlying traumas this student had, our young 5th grader found himself in a mandatory placement situation where he was to be away from our campus for at least 45 days.

Within those 45 days, of course, both students and teachers felt they were given the solace and peace needed to recover from all the chaos. And I'm not saying that any of them were wrong for feeling such a way. But once the realization that the 45 days were coming to an end, I knew that I would need to do some major Preparation and Prevention. Because within those 45 days, I had visited with that 5th grader, spent time talking to him and preparing him for his transition. One major component of that was his support plan, of which I was definitely included, but so was a handful of other adults. Therefore, I knew that in order for him to be successful, I would have to make sure that everyone was on the same page.

Remember before I stated that *this work is for the kids, but it is really about the adults*.

He was eager and excited to return to campus, and I wanted to ensure that I kept him encouraged and with that same attitude for the days to come. But in order to be able to do that, I had to include his teachers as well as his classmates.

In the few days before his return, I conducted a Re-entry Circle[32] with his peers a restorative practice that is often overlooked but is SO critical to bringing everyone together in a way that the culture becomes one in which all voices are honored and shown to be interconnected. At the end, you want and need everyone to know that their voice matters, their feelings are valid, but most importantly, every person is worthy-even those who make poor choices.

On the day of his return, we had a Circle of Support and Accountability (COSA),[33] which consisted of his support team: me, the counselor, and Administrator, his teachers, his connected adult, and his parent. (a COSA script can be found on my website).

I would say the Circle was a success, both of them. And for a few weeks, so was the support plan. But consistency is the name of the game. And for those familiar with FBA/ABA, you know that behaviors follow certain pathways, and everyone has to be willing to weather the ups-and-downs, the plateaus, and the pushing of buttons. And sadly, for this particular student, the majority of people around him were unwilling, unable, and/or unequipped to provide this 5th grade student with all he needed because he was sent away again- almost immediately.

32 A Re-entry Circle is a type of Circle used once a person has been removed from an environment for an extended period of time. This absence can be from an illness, hospitalization, suspension, relocation, etc.

33 Circle of Support and Accountability (COSA): a Circle that involves members of a community that will act as a support system for a person who needs additional resources and/or has returned from a prolonged absence.

And I realize that I am oversimplifying much of this story which doesn't really do this story justice, but I was compelled to use this anecdote for this chapter because I will never forget what he said right before he left:

"I told you Ms. Hardy. Don't nobody want me here. I felt it as soon as I walked back through the doors."

Shared Experience Moment

Think of a student you had that struggled with choices, whether academically or socially.

- What needs of the student were not being met? What needs of yours were not being met that prevented you from supporting/engaging more?
- Now in retrospect, are there moments that could have played out differently?
- What have you learned from this student that you can use in the future?
- How did this experience prepare you for future disappointments?

Restorative Recipe #10
Remember it's a Marathon,
not a Sprint

—

Ross W. Greene, the author of *Lost at School: Why Our Kids with Behavioral Challenges are Falling Through the Cracks and How We Can Help Them*, states: *Challenging behavior* occurs when the demands and expectations being placed upon a child outstrip the skills he has to respond adaptively."[34]

Too often in our educational organizations, we react instead of respond. Thus, sometimes without even realizing, we are operating in a hyperactive state within an upside-down triangle. For the student I referenced for this chapter, much of what we did was a reaction to, instead of an intentional response using the plan we had collaboratively put together. My 5th grader, just like many other babies who display Tier III behaviors, did consume lots of time from the adults on campus. And at times it was exhaustive. We have all been guilty of celebrating the days when a particular student is absent. However, let me be clear, he did not live in "Tier III land" at every moment of the day-none of our students do. Which is why it is key to have a wide, solid foundation/base of that triangle so that you can build on an effective support system. Only within a supportive community can accountability take place. The building of positive and appropriate relationships is ongoing and constant, not just limited to a responsive approach to addressing incidents.

In the anecdote, I mentioned a Re-entry Circle, as well as a Circle of Support and Accountability (COSA); both are for- mal Tier III Restorative practice. Allow me to emphasize that the facilitation of these types of Circles needs to have a Circle Keeper/ facilitator that has been trained in working with conflict, harm, and trauma. And not just a few hours of training, but the mindset has to be present, and experience needs to be apparent. There are so many moving pieces before, during, and after these types of Circles, that one must know each step of the process thoroughly- same as the Harm/Conflict Circle previously discussed. Without proper training, there is a risk of creating more harm.

COSAs can assist in transforming conflict. *Transforming conflict* means addressing the immediate situation and *at the same time* building capacity to strengthen relationships.[35] It provides an opportunity for the 'responsible youth' to make things right in such a way that it goes above and beyond the negative labels and identity that is often attached to those who cause

34 https://www.azquotes.com/author/95458-Ross_W_Greene

35 Evans, K., and D. Vaandering. 2016. *The Little Book of Restorative Justice in Education, Fostering Responsibility, Healing, and Hope in Schools.* 93. New York, NY: Good Books Publishing

harm, while simultaneously allowing the system of support to put a Restorative Action Plan (RAP)[36] in place to meet the needs of not only the 'responsible youth', but the community at large. The RAP should:

- be created during the Re-entry meeting
- include the strengths or positive attributes
- include support members
- have detailed steps of implementation (dates, locations,
- times, people)
- set a follow-up meeting date to celebrate progress and
- revise the plan if necessary
- be distributed to all pertinent individuals, including students and parent/guardian
- make sure that the expectations of making things as
- right is possible is clear and stated directly

When the one who caused harm is made a part of the solution also helps to highlight the assets and positives that the student brings to the campus- which reinforces the idea of belonging and connection. As previously stated, all of us desire to be in relationships- and positive ones, not negative.

---

36 Restorative Action Plan is a document that details support, goals, timelines, and other information in support of the reintegration of someone who has been away for an extended period of time

As previously stated, all of us desire to be in relationships- and positive ones, not negative. So, involving the 'responsible youth' in the solutions not only reinforces the positive relationship sought out, but also intrinsically motivates the student to follow the planned practices. This also reinforces all five of the CASEL components, particularly 'Responsible Decision-making' and 'Self-regulation' skills as the student has direct involvement and choice.

Re-entry Circles can also transform conflict as it serves as a way for all those impacted by the actions of the 'responsible youth' to express their thoughts and feelings, but just as important, it creates a space to build empathy for that person as well as think about the supports needed for everyone to exist without fear or intentional harm. During these discussions, you want to find out what is motivating the inappropriate behaviors. Or what some may know as the 'Function of Behavior'- which is a part of the FBA process. All behavior is a means of communication, and every behavior is motivated by two functions: to get something or avoid something. So, making sure to meet the need of the function will usually extinguish the misbehavior. We need to take the time to decipher the message in order to be able to guide students on a different path of choices that will help in a student's desire to want to change their behavior. We can't just simply label misbehaviors and assign punishments. Nor tell them exactly what to do.

One quick example that comes to mind is kicking students out of the classroom. When students are removed from any setting for inappropriate behavior, they quickly learn that doing A or B, will allow them to leave. After quickly realizing that traditional punitive measures will get them out of class, students will continue to misbehave and take advantage for their own purposes. However, leaving takes away any accountability to the setting and those in it and it, ultimately, reinforces the function of their behavior through the misbehaviors-which is the opposite effect we want. Educators need to stop sending students away.

Yes, I know I went a little out of the realm of restorative, however, being mindful and intentional about this is key. And just as other Circles, the format for these types of Circles do not change, but the 'Discussion Round' questions will, as these questions are based on the purpose of the Circle.

RAPs can and should also be created when a student is removed from the classroom for a short period of time temporarily or a full class period, which is a common occurrence. It usually does not require a full Re-entry Circle process, but a conference should still take place with possibly the Counselor, Administrator, or other person in charge of discipline or all three. In this meeting, you want to ask the same Restorative Questions. Before returning to class or the environment removed, you need to make sure that the adult(s) are mentally and/or emotionally prepared to have that person back. Too often, I had an extremely productive conversation with a student, promoting optimism and hopes, only to have been dramatically proven wrong the moment the door opens- which happened to the student in my story. Therefore, in order to keep the relationships from immediately deteriorating even more, make sure the adults are ready. Ask them what they need in order to have that student back. This also helps solidify the relationship between the adults as every person is being acknowledged.

So, within this meeting, you want to discuss different scenarios that the student could encounter from their peers and, possibly, the adult(s). Role-play responses so that there is some preparation which will help with emotions. Talk about how to ask for help or what to do to self-regulate. Then inform the adult(s) of what was discussed and what the plan is. It might be helpful to talk to the adult first prior to returning the youth, so that you can make sure the environment is welcoming. The adult has to be on board! And they must know this. And know that their attitude and actions can either help or harm. Hopefully, by this time of requiring this type of interaction that a solid base of Restorative Values, Practices, and Beliefs exist so that the process is embraced rather than rejected.

We know that no human is perfect. Everyone- adults and youth alike- makes mistakes. And mistakes should be used as an opportunity to learn and develop skills and

....

abilities that Dr. Konopka, as cited by Nancy Riestenberg, asserts that all young people need, which include the need to:

- participate as citizens, as members if a household, as
- workers, and as responsible members of society
- gain experience in decision-making
- interact with peers
- reflect on self in relation to others and discover self by
- looking outward as well as inward
- discuss conflicting values and formulate their own value
- system
- experiment with their own identity and with
- relationships
- try out various roles without having to commit them-
- selves irrevocably
- develop a feeling of accountability in the context of a relationship among equals
- cultivate a capacity to enjoy life
- participate in the creative arts, learn self-expression,
- and communicate deeper feelings from within[37,38]

---

37 Ristenberg, N. 2012. *Circle in the Square Building Community and Repairing Harm in School.* 42-43. St. Paul, MN: Living Justice Press
38 Konopka, G. "Requirements of Healthy Development of Adolescent Youth",
Adolescence 8, no. 31: (Fall 1973): 20

....

When traditional methods are used and students are not properly reintegrated into the school community, opportunities to develop and acquire skills are critically missed. And a violation of a rule, should not deprive any one the opportunity to grow. But "traditional soil" still does just that. And if the 'responsible youth' does not believe in their own ability to transform behavior, then he or she will continue to be stagnant, believing that the past will determine their future. Which is why I encourage and urge educators to shift their thinking and take the path that leads to 'Restorative'.

Yet I know, establishing a restorative school culture is not easy and change does not occur overnight it takes years. But if you continue down the restorative path, trust me, the transformation will be all worth it. Circles are truly a power move, even though they can take a length of time, which is the only con if there is one to consider. But as Pam Leo, author of \Connection *Parenting* states:

"Either we spend time meeting children's emotional needs by filling their cup with love or we spend time dealing with the behaviors caused from their unmet needs. Either way, we spend the time."[39]

---

39. Leo, P. https://www.goodreads.com/author/show/329779.Pam_Leo

It's So Hard to Say Goodbye
Crunch Time
May

—

May is always bittersweet. The bitterness lies in all the testing: standardized, AP, EOC. In all the deadlines of meeting IEP requirements, drills that were postponed, and all the tons of grading that never made it out of that pile in the corner or your trunk. Students are desperately asking for extra credit or tutoring sessions. Or those who see no hope are all the way mentally checked out. Just about everyone's capacity is full, while racing towards the finish line. It is quite a stressful time.

On the sweet side, 5th, 8th grade, and Seniors are doing all of their last activities, while other grades are also enjoying those final moments of that chapter in their life. Yearbooks are being signed. Phone numbers and social media handles are being shared. TikToks and Reels are being created. And the relief of not having the same stressors, triggers, and pressures of the school year, but instead summertime fun (for most) or the idea of nothingness, resonates through the hallways.

And for the past 10 months, you and your students have been building a community, a family, a team, that will have life-long lasting effects. In order to acknowledge and honor this moment, here are a few activities I would do at the end of every year:

1. Appreciation Circle- The entire class gets into a large circle. You will need yarn. Let the students know that each student in the class will be appreciated and to make sure that this happens, everyone must raise their hand. Only when someone has acknowledged you, are you able to put your hand down. No one can be acknowledged more than once. And the goal is to say something-anything-that is positive. After that, each person is to hold onto their piece of yarn before tossing it to the next student. As the adult in the room, you will be the last person to be appreciated to ensure that all students are shown appreciation. You ask if anyone would like to start, and then you acknowledge that person as you toss them the ball of yarn-this will eliminate the dilemma of students having their feelings hurt over you choosing a student to start with (I sadly had to learn the hard and sad way about this one). Once the first student chooses someone, the process continues until the last student has only you as an option to appreciate.

One year, I remember, I had a student who was definitely socially awkward as he struggled to make genuine connections with his peers and his teachers. This student usually had strict, conservative, narrow-minded perspectives of the world that sometimes-bordered racism and misogyny. And to be honest, the stuff that would come out of his mouth the majority of the time, was low-key rude, disrespectful, and sometimes hurtful. He even once indirectly threatened to stab me with a knife! However, despite all of this, the classroom culture we had built was *SO STRONG* that we all allowed him to be who he was, accepted him in the community still, and treated him with dignity and respect, even when he struggled to reciprocate. Trust me though it was not an easy road, but honestly, he and that class became one of my most prized accomplishments.

So back to how this connects to the Appreciation Circle...

As the yarn is bouncing around the Circle and the options of students is getting less and less, I look over to the student above mentioned and could see the anxiety in his eyes. It's now down to the second to the last student who has the ball of yarn and is scanning the Circle looking for raised hands. Once she realizes the only one left was this particular student, she takes a deep breath and then says, "B, I want to appreciate you for always bringing a different perspective into the classroom," and tosses him the yarn. He thanks her, gives a slight smile, and then scans the Circle and then proceeds to say, "Ms. Hardy, no one is left." I then say, "That's not true. I am left." And when I tell you the whole room fell silent and then, almost in slow motion, like a movie, it seemed like everyone simultaneously looked from me to him, holding their breath, anticipating his next move. It was no secret about the threat to me and his consequence (he was suspended), so needless to say, our relationship was definitely fractured.

He stands there for a few seconds, staring down at the ground, twirling the ball of yarn in his hands. Then he takes a deep breath and begins to mumble inaudible words. "B, toss me the ball of yarn first please and then speak a little louder because I don't think any of us can hear you." He tosses me the ball of yarn from across the Circle and takes another deep breath before speaking again.

"Ms. Hardy... [long pause]... I want to say... ummm... thank you, I guess, for ummm...teaching us. I've actually learned a lot."

"Thank you, B. That is very nice of you to say, and I truly appreciate you sharing that with me, with all of us." With surprise and shock still plainly on everyone's face, some- one started to "slow clap". Which soon turned into a thunderous roar of claps, and cheers, as everyone in the Circle began to praise B for his participation and appreciation. It truly was a beautiful, authentic moment that perfectly ended the school year.

2. Envelope Notes- This is an activity I would do in my Advisory class, but you could do it for all your classes if you wish and/ or have the space.

Give each student a letter envelope to decorate, on both sides, or at least a name on the backside where the opening is. Feel free to make one for you too. Then have all the envelopes displayed somewhere with the flap part facing outward so that items can be placed in them. Pass out index cards (or can use lined paper) and have students cut them in half or in fours and then instruct each student to make/create a note for EACH student. Of course, remind students (a few times) of the expectations of the type of note and content that are appropriate. I used to tell them to write down things that could be read in public, in front of adults- their parents or guardians. Then you can either trust students will meet those expectations, or you can glance over the notes, but do not read them. Remember you have spent the entire year building trust and setting boundaries-you don't want to violate or fracture relationships by being intrusive in the last moments.

Once finished, have the students count out the number of notes written which should match the number of students in your class (minus themselves) or at least 90%. Why all the students, you ask? Well, you never want anyone to be left out. At any moment. We do not get to choose our students, students do not get to choose their classmates, so regardless of the different dynamics and levels of relationships, everyone belongs to your classroom community/ family- a lesson that will also prepare them for the real world.

3. Grade level party- Now I understand the difficulty this may pose for some campuses depending on the structure, but if you find a way to bring the

grade levels together or acad- emies for a final community-building activity, I can almost guarantee it will be a memory worth creating.

All throughout the school year, I emphasized the phrase 'Team 9' as I, and my whole grade level team, wanted to emphasize our unity. And so, we started the tradition of having the 'Team 9 Ceremony' at the end of the year. Here, we gave out awards based mostly in character traits and growth mindset.[40] We did community-building activities that allowed the kids to interact, and we would even make time for students to share some of their final thoughts and/ or feelings.

Sidenote about a Growth Mindset: As authors Maynard and Weinstein describe, "the first step toward helping students build a growth mindset is boosting their confidence. Many students misbehave because they don't feel successful academically. If we can build their confidence, the behavior will often take care of itself...Students need to believe in their capacity to change and succeed before they will fully invest effort in whatever skill they're trying to master."[41] Failing forward is the goal.

People have to know that there are multiple opportunities to experience success. An environment that promotes and focuses on growth mindset will definitely have more success with establishing a restorative community because those who have a fixed mindset are less likely to take accountability for their behavior or embrace restorative practices as a whole. Students need to know that they can better themselves- that who they are in that particular moment is not who they always have to be-change is possible. I have a poster that I used to display in my class- room and then in my office that read: Every expert was once a beginner. And I love this because it is a reminder that no one is 100% at any given thing without hard work and dedication. That effort is critical part of the process and that it's okay not to "get it" right away. Also, offering personal stories about your own journeys of growth, and finding a way for students to reflect on their life, is a powerful way to solidify a growth mindset environment.

I will never forget one year where one student, who was not the best academically, so he struggled with making it through 9th grade and even considered dropping out- thoughts only a few people were aware of. But at this ceremony, he shared some of his most intimate inner feelings that focused on how no matter how much he messed up or didn't believe in him- self, he had teachers and other students who would encourage him to try again the next day.

---

40 A growth mindset is when a person believes that you are not stuck with the idea that intelligence, talent, and character cannot be changed (fixed).
41 Maynard N. and Weinstein B. 89. *Hacking School Discipline 9 Ways to Create a Culture of Empathy & Responsibility and Using Restorative Justice.* 2020. Highland Heights, OH. Times Ten Publication.

To take each day one at a time. And he expressed how much that meant to him. There wasn't a dry eye in the place. Until he then, courageously, professed his love for one of the female students he had known for a long time and then everyone exploded in cheers and congratulations. She wasn't interested, and he said that was ok, because 10 months ago, he would have never had the bravery to do such a thing, but the family we had built let him know he was in a safe space and that no one would ridicule or make jokes. This is a moment that definitely lives rent-free in my mind.

Asking our students, and even ourselves, to stretch beyond the realms of our comfort zones is not an easy thing, and shifting a mindset definitely takes intention and consistency, but the reward is definitely worth it. It's nothing like the feeling of a safe space. Hopefully, after implementing this will be evident by the end of the school year.

Shared Experience Moment

What activities do you and your students do in those final moments of the school year?

- How do you balance the stress as well as the connection?
- Are there any "special moments" that have occurred?

Restorative Recipe #11
Appreciate & Celebrate All of the Work

—

Congratulations! The end of the school year has arrived, and you have survived! But honestly, my hope is that you and your students did more than just survive. I hope that you all thrived and am transitioning into the next phase of life better than when you started the one before it, mainly because you are now rooted in Restorative soil, living within the core values

(which all begin with 'r'):

- Respect (foundation)
- Relationships (roots)
- Responsibility
- Repair
- Reintegration

Keeping these values in combination with social-emotional teaching and trauma-informed care and practices, and you have the recipe for positive school culture and lasting change.

Remember these Ingredients:

- ✓ Relationships over Rules
- ✓ Your mindset must shift
- ✓ Punitive and Exclusionary methods are

counterproductive and do not teach
- ✓ Social-Emotional Skills are learned
- ✓ Find the positive first and praise and acknowledge it
- ✓ Teaching beyond content is a part of your responsibility
- ✓ There is Power in Circle
- ✓ Empathy is one of the most valuable character traits to develop
- ✓ Make the Time
- ✓ Brain development and age-appropriate behavior always need consideration
- ✓ Consider the 'iceberg': Understand the story
- ✓ Learn the motivation and function of the behavior before deciding consequences and/or interventions
- ✓ There are adults who struggle with problem solving and conflict resolution, so please give our babies a break
- ✓ Show yourself grace as well
- ✓ Professional Development should not just be a "1-off"
- ✓ True change in culture takes 3-5 years

Summer, Summer, Summertime June/July

—

As with the feeling of almost all educators, summer break is   a time needed and well-deserved. The number of unpaid hours of work along with the mental and emotional exhaustion, definitely calls for an adult beverage on a tropical island somewhere.

But for a handful of us, summers are short-lived by the need to work summer school.

I worked summer school one year only because two of my closest friends were teaching too. They were a part of my 'Teacher Squad'- a necessary group of fellow teachers that you could eat lunch with, vent with, send students to, share ideas with, give pep talks to, and have pep talks given, coordinate on Spirit days, text during PDs, and support and love on. Overall, they were more than work friends to me and so spending 6 weeks of my summer with them seemed like a great idea. Plus, when I found out what my check was also going to be looking like, I decided to forego my much-needed rest.

For those who have taught summer school before, you know that your class consists of students who may come from other schools and that you are expected to teach 10 weeks of information in half the time. Needless to say, maintaining a restorative mindset proved difficult.

I remember during my abridged version of my 'Drink the Water' speech, I included directives that sounded much more authoritative than not.

"I am not here as a babysitter for you this summer," I stated. "I am here to teach you lots of information in a short period of time, which means that I have no tolerance for the shenanigans. If you do not want to be here or know you are not commit- ted to doing your best, then please enjoy your summer and try again next school year."

Remember that I stated that no one lives in one tier of the triangle, no one square of the matrix; we are fluid. So, although my stated expectations were not as restorative, in hindsight, as they could have been, I feel that my expectations were clear. And I was dedicated to helping each one of them get to a passing grade.

What I experienced that summer though actually surprised me, because although my initial delivery may have been more on the traditional side, my lessons and how I taught them were very much aligned with who I was, who I still am, as an educator and that is 'restorative' at heart. I had already witnessed the impact of how a restorative community and interpersonal connections could transform lives with my prior students, so as I taught my lessons, I made sure to make sure to make time still to have Circle and spend time getting to know one another beyond the surface.

At the end of the 6 weeks, students who were once

strangers became friends and I had a new set of babies to look after. I realized that even in a short period of time, relationships and connections were possible and so when the opportunity came to teach the Summer Bridge program for the incoming 9th graders, I eagerly jumped at the opportunity- which also turned out to be the best 3 weeks of my summer that year and for the summer after that. Summer Bridge was an opportunity to start building relationships early which created a community from the very first day. We had Juniors and Seniors assist with the awesome project students worked on as well as with the com- munity-building activities such as the Community Walk and School Tour. And when the official first day of school began, you could literally feel the difference. I encourage all schools to have such a program, especially if the goal is to build a restorative community.

Shared Experience Moment

How do you usually spend your summer?

- What are some ways that you spend restoring yourself?
- How do you spend time preparing for the next school year to come?

Restorative Recipe #12
Reflection

—

By this point, my hope is that you feel not only better educated about all things Restorative, but also that you feel confident and rejuvenated about your teaching and this profession as a whole. Equally, I hope that you spend time taking care of yourself genuinely. I know how easy it is to become burnt out or cold- hearted when it seems that the art of teaching is constantly under attack, usually by those who have never taught in a classroom. But please know that the work you do matters.

You matter. And it matters the most to the babies you impact on a daily basis.

Remember to always be intentional in not only what you teach, but more importantly *how* you teach. Because although traditionalists would believe that academics should come first, and then behavior should follow, the reality is that learning hap- pens best when amazing relationships exist. And that also takes intentionality. Relationship skills *have* to be taught as well as practiced, so that all students of all backgrounds, ages, nation- alities, and ethnic groups can benefit from a school environment where relationships matter. A school that recognizes that people and the relationships that exist amongst its stakeholders are the bases of both learning and safety.

Remember to be an advocate for inclusion and unity. In today's day and age, so many of our marginalized groups are being placed even more on the fringes of society as DEI, African- American history and contribution, gender affirmation, and LGBTQ+ are all under attack and scrutiny. It is a MORAL judgment to disregard any of these groups. And just because you make a statement of fact such as, "gay people exist in this world and should be treated with respect" does not mean you are promoting homosexuality- you are simply honoring one's humanity. And that should always be in the forefront of your mind while educating. Students pay attention to not only what you say, but also to everything you don't.

Also Remember, during this time to allow for your mental and emotional health to recalibrate and for your physical body to rest and reset. I think we take for granted how much energy it takes to do what we do and the toll it can take.

And Also Remember, that even after reading this book and participating in trainings, the beginning implementation stages of Restorative will not be the magic wand or the fairy dust that you may want. You have to read and study, practice, learn from the mistakes and hard times, review and evaluate. Most importantly though, it requires buy-in from the entire school or organization for it to truly thrive. But please do not allow that to deter you from continuing down the Restorative path, you can start small and expand-that's how I did. As long as you are intentional and consistent, and not just 'do' Restorative, but 'LIVE' Restorative, your best days are for sure going to come. Things will change when your mindset does.

This book is intended to provide not only hope, but also realness of what is possible as someone who was once in your shoes. I want to believe that my stories were relatable and personable, but also realistic in the sense of being plausible. I encourage you to discuss, further research, explore, test, and question, all the information, theories, and ideas provided. But my ultimate wish is for you take the leap of faith and make that Restorative shift!

I often miss the days that I spent in the classroom because the bonds that were cemented are difficult to come by when you do not have a classroom of your own to grow and nurture every day. The connections and legacies with those babies continue though as I have been invited to baby showers, weddings, college graduations. I know that what we did in our classroom mattered and it wasn't necessarily the content, but it was the relationships. And all those special moments and times where our humanity shined. I know for so many of them, because they have said it themselves, that experiencing Circle and living within a Restorative Community put their lives on a vastly different path. Which, for me, is the greatest honor.

In addition to all of that, however, I also know that this

book, my trainings, and the content I post, allow me to sprinkle a little of myself on others so that our youth and adults alike can be impacted on a grander scale. And that brings me tremendous joy!

So, if you find yourself wanting to continue this journey with me, please reach out! I would love to support you and/ or your organization. And if not, that's disappointing, but I do encourage you to continue a journey of life-learning and to not fall complacent to the "traditional" soil your organization resides. We all benefit from continuous growth. And Restorative Practices can grow our community into something beyond our highest expectations.

References

Affective Statement Practice.

https://www.restorativeresources.org/uploads/5/6/1/4/561430 33/affective_statements_practice.pdf

Boyes-Watson, C., and K. Pranis. 2015. Circle Forward, 139. St. Paul, MN: Living Justice Press

Burnett, N., and M. Thorsborne. 2015. Restorative Practice and Special Needs, 60. Philadelphia, PA: Jessica Kingsley Publishers

Classen, R., and Classen, R. 2008. Discipline that Restores. South Carolina: BookSurge Publishing.

Classen, R., and Classen, R. 2015. Making Things Right: Activities that teach restorative justice, conflict resolutions, mediation, and discipline that restores. North Charleston, SC: Book Surge Publishing.

Evans, K., and D. Vaandering. 2016. The Little Book of Restorative Justice in Education, Fostering Responsibility, Healing, and Hope in Schools. 28. 93. New York, NY: Good Books Publishing

Fisher, N. and Fisher, D. and Smith, D. 2015. Better Than Carrots or Sticks Restorative Practices for Positive Classroom Management. 9. 18-19. Alexandria, VA: ASCD

Hendry, R.

https://www.azquotes.com/author/95458-Ross_W_Greene

https://www.goodreads.com/author/show/329779.Pam_Leo

Ierley, A. and Ivker, C. "Restoring School Communities: A Report on the

Colorado Restorative Justice in Schools Program," Research and Practice Insert, Voma

Connections 13 (Winter 2003); Legal Rights Center Grantee Report, 2011

Konopka, G. "Requirements of Healthy Development of Adolescent

. . . .

169

Youth", Adolescence 8, no. 31: (Fall 1973): 20

Maynard N. and Weinstein B. 24. 89. 102. Hacking School Discipline 9 Ways to Create a Culture of Empathy & and; Responsibility and Using Restorative Justice. 2020. Highland Heights, OH. Times Ten Publication.

Pranis, K. 2003. Peacemaking Circles: from crime to community. St. Paul, MN. Living Justice Press

Ristenberg, N. 2012. Circle in the Square Building Community and Repairing Harm in School. 30. 42-43. 75. 108. St. Paul, MN: Living Justice Press

Sprague, J., and Nelson, C.M. School-wide Positive Behavior Interventions and Supports and restorative discipline in schools.

https://pages.uoregon.edu/ivdb/documents/RJ%20and%20PBIS%20Mo nograph%20for%20OSEP%2010

The Advancement Project. 2010. Federal Policy, ESEA Reauthorization, and the School to Prison Pipeline.

What is the CASEL Framework? **https://casel.org/fundamentals-of-sel/what-**is-the-casel-framework.

Zehr, H. 1990. Changing lenses: A new focus for crime and justice. Scottdale, PA: Herald Press.

Zehr, H. The Little Book of Restorative Justice. 2002. Intercourse, PA. Good Books.